TRANSFORMED BY LOVE

STORIES OF URBAN MINISTRY

Elizabeth K Ellis

Published by Cliff Street Books

cliffstreetbooks@twcny.rr.com

ISBN-13: 978-1-7353633-2-5
Library of Congress Control Number: 2024915083
First Paperback Printing: August, 2024

Cover Photograph by Sharon Gunther
Book Design by Joshua Adams

CLIFF STREET BOOKS
Ithaca, NY 14850

TABLE OF CONTENTS

ACKNOWLEDGEMENTS

Writing this book, and then publishing it, has been a long process. There have been so many stops and starts along the way. It first began with a writing group here in Philadelphia, organized by the Reverend Beverly Dale (Dale to her friends!) After an initial meeting, the group which includes Amy Mann, Lauri Perman, and Dale met, worked, and prayed together for over ten years. The interfaith nature of the group—Jewish, Quaker and Protestant—was especially enriching. There would be no book without them. They have given encouragements, critiques, cheers, and inspiration for all of this time, and sometimes they have had to push me! Thank you, friends. I am blessed.

There have been people who have read the book and given extremely helpful feedback including "Holy Spirits" Scotty McLennan, Anita Farber-Robinson, and the late Thomas Mikelson, colleagues in the ministry and the spiritual life through the years. Another colleague, Alison Cornish, read and generously offered excellent feedback. Early in the process a professor friend of my son's, Lauren Cattaneo of George Mason University, whom I have yet to meet, read the manuscript and shared her wisdom and insight to give me great feedback. At one point in the journey the book was in process with another publisher, and Marshall Hawkins, the editor there, made a significant contribution to the manuscript, working with me over time. The book and I have benefited greatly from these friends and their wisdom.

I have tried to combine two main themes, the stories, lives, and challenges of people in low-income neighborhoods of cities, and my own spiritual journey in doing ministry there. I would not have had these opportunities if I had not been called to the Benevolent Fraternity of Unitarian Churches in 1978, hired by the Reverend Virgil Bud Murdock, and later to continue urban ministry in Chester, Pennsylvania, hired to work at Pendle Hill by Steve Baumgarten. These people believed in the mission and me and gave me opportunity and support. During a difficult time of transition at the UU Urban Ministry, I was strongly and compassionately supported by Board president, Ned Leibensperger and the Unitarian Universalist Department of Ministry director, David Hubner.

And this is a spiritual journey that I have not traveled alone. Lou Lipps SJ offered me the first experience of compassionate spiritual direction at a critical time. George Drury, SJ introduced me to the Ignatian way and provided me with spiritual direction for many years and all manner of experiences. "The Holy Spirit moves in freedom" he often said. John Kerdiejus SJ directed me in the Spiritual Exercises of Saint Ignatius, with compassion, skill, and humor. Early in my studies, Dr. James Fowler was my advisor and inspiration in my independent study program and his advice and wisdom shaped my ministry in many ways. Other directors on retreat or in transitions have helped me listen to the Spirit. My present director, Rev. Joseph Schaller continues in this journey, wisely accompanying me through the present challenges. A wonderful psychotherapist, Dr. Pamela Geib helped me through several, often tumultuous years in Boston, and certainly qualifies as a spiritual influence because she always saw and spoke to my deepest being.

And there is family—my children, Lee Adams and Rachel Ellis Adams, have been constantly supportive and encouraging over the years of this process, as has been my longtime friend and companion, Sharon Gunther, who helped me to be at home in Pennsylvania, and continually inspires me with her artist's vision. My former husband and good friend, Rev. Graylan Hagler taught me much about urban ministry and continues to educate me in justice work. And I owe infinite gratitude to Joshua Adams, my stepson, who has published this manuscript, and created a book. There would be no book without him. Thank you, Joshua. I am blessed with exceptional people in my life, and I appreciate it.

There is no way, of course, to acknowledge and appreciate the multitude of people who have influenced this book by their very being. This includes the people whose stories I tell and the many others whose important stories I have witnessed. It also includes the many "workers in the vineyard," the volunteers, the frontline workers, the ministers. You are in my cells, my breath, my soul and I love you. Thank you.

Finally, this is a journey of faith and all along the way, through bright times and dark ones, I have been touched, sustained, and guided by the nameless one with many names, Holy Mystery, Holy Spirit, God beyond God, that ineffable, eternal, transcendent truth of Love.

INTRODUCTION

It was one of many late-night calls. A guest in Renewal House, a confidential shelter for women in crisis, was acting erratic, threatening other guests and the night-time staff person. I knew the woman to be delicately balanced but, after all, she was more than eight months pregnant. "What are we going to do?" I thought, as I hurried over to the shelter. "Insist that she leave? Pregnant and homeless?" As often happens in the ministry, matters took care of themselves that night. As soon as I walked in the door of the shelter, the woman shouted and then doubled up with a severe labor pain. We rushed to the hospital, her water breaking in my car. I left her with the emergency room staff and by the time I had parked my car and returned, a new baby had been born. The mother was now calm, and they would return to Renewal House for a brief period before moving into a new home. This little boy was one of many babies born while their mothers sought shelter and long-term safe homes—little people born into a world of struggle and the infinite hopefulness of new beginnings. Their lives, like so many others, have touched mine, briefly but importantly, during my time ministering in neighborhoods of the city.

This is my story of ministry in diverse, low-income communities. It is the story of people met and loved during twenty-three years at the UU Urban Ministry in Boston, and during continuing years in Pennsylvania. Many of my "urban parishioners" struggled with poverty, violence, or drug addiction. Some of them would overcome the conditions that prevented them from being fully the people that God intended. Some would not. But all of these lives were important, each one a precious child of the Holy with absolute worth and dignity. I was privileged to be their minister.

In the 1970s I was the director of religious education at First Parish in Lexington, Massachusetts when I felt the call to what I initially thought was parish ministry. A single parent with financial responsibilities, I applied to and was accepted into a Unitarian Universalist Association (UUA) independent study program for parish ministry, which would enable me to study part-time and continue my work at First Parish. I was in for a major transformation: during my first class at Harvard Divinity School—The Sociology of Religion—I was introduced to liberation theology, and I knew immediately and deeply that my ministerial call was not to the parish, but to the larger community. I wished to minister with people who were struggling for justice and equitable lives. I was inspired by the professor, Sr. Marie Augusta Neal, SNDdeN, who said, among many memorable things, "People go to the country to find God because God is too hard to take in the city." For me, however, I realized that it was the God of the city that called me clearly and joyfully. I could not imagine what form such a ministry could take, but I knew that was where I wished to be.

In 1978, after a wonderful ordination at the Lexington church, I was exceedingly fortunate to be called as associate minister at large with the Benevolent Fraternity of Unitarian Churches (affectionately nicknamed the "Ben Frat"), now doing business as the UU Urban Ministry. (My name at that time was Elizabeth, or Betty, Adams.) Founded in 1826 by the Reverend Doctor Joseph Tuckerman, the primary mission of this Boston agency is to help those who are poor in the city by providing a ministry at large—that is, with ministers in the community rather than in a particular church. The shape of this at-large ministry at any given time depends on the needs of the community and the vision and resources of the particular ministry team. Through the years, the work has taken place in chapels, settlement houses, summer camps, prisons, and shelters, and it has included a legal ministry, community organizing, ministry with immigrants, and more.

When people think of ministers they automatically think "church." In fact, when I had my interview with the UUA's Ministerial Fellowship Committee, the credentialing body for Unitarian Universalist ministers, they listened to my desire to work in community with marginalized people, warmly wished me good luck, and fellowshipped me for parish ministry. Community ministry within the UUA has received greater recognition in recent years and there are many today who serve in a variety of non-church situations.

In this book I tell the stories of some of my urban parishioners and the particular challenges they faced. This is also the story of my own growth in ministry: my spiritual growth through tragedy and success, through losing and finding, through my own weaknesses, and through God's great mercy.

During the first years of the ministry at large I worked with others to create Renewal House, a confidential shelter for women in crisis, especially victims of domestic violence. I had been called to the Benevolent Fraternity in a partnership with the Franklin Square House, a Universalist nonprofit housing corporation founded by the Reverend George Perin in 1902, originally organized to provide safe, supervised housing in the city for women. By the 1970s, women were no longer seeking such housing, so the Franklin Square House was looking for a new way to fulfill its purpose. They agreed to my proposal to donate space for a shelter for women in crisis, to be created and run by the Benevolent Fraternity.

During the first year of my ministry, I used that shelter as overflow space for another shelter, Casa Myrna. I learned the ropes by volunteering there and made connections in my neighborhood. I called this activity the Franklin Square Ministry. In addition to overflow from Casa Myrna, in those first months I took in a number of women facing different kinds of crises.

By 1980 a significant community of women was volunteering in this effort, and we opened a full-time shelter for women in crisis, naming it Renewal House. The lives and stories of the shelter's guests make up the first part of this book: the emancipated minor who strip-danced in the firehouse; the alcoholic woman who tried to free herself from violence and addiction; the wife of an abusive former soldier who fled with her child to safety in the shelter.

The second section includes stories from a storefront church where I was involved with my former husband and good friend, the Rev. Graylan Hagler (we were then Ellis-Hagler). The church was a joint denominational effort supported by the UUA, the United Church of Christ (UCC), and the Christian Church (Disciples of Christ). It was the Disciples that initially encouraged us and gave us the first grant. Because of a large daily Narcotics Anonymous meeting in the building, this very diverse congregation included a large number of people recovering from addiction. Their stories involved tragedy as well as courage and inspiration. The experience of preaching, praying, and pastoring in such an expressive group influenced my ministry for years to come. Their openness and courage helped me to see the patterns of addiction in my own life and later to seek the help of a twelve-step recovery group.

In 1987, I became the senior minister and executive director of the Benevolent Fraternity, then doing business as the UU Urban Ministry (UUUM). Soon after, there was a series of tragic gang-related shootings in the neighborhood surrounding the First Church in Roxbury, an historically important church site that had legally merged into the UUUM. When the crack epidemic and consequent youth gang wars of the early 1990s broke out, we hired a gang outreach worker and then invited our local gang into the church building. After setting rules and boundaries, we welcomed the young people every night of the school week for dinner and to participate in alternatives-to-violence programming. In the coming years I came to know some of these young people well and as minister at large made regular visits to them in prison and hospitals. Sadly, the time included funerals as well. Stories of these young people make up the third section of the book.

Some of the stories I tell are tragic. I tell them because each of these lives is precious and deserves to be known, and the conditions which have led to the sad endings need to be changed. Some of the social conditions that give rise to the problems touched on in this book have actually gotten worse. Public health officials have recently declared that the current opioid epidemic is the worst drug crisis in history. During a recent pandemic, domestic violence cases increased significantly, and Philadelphia experienced its highest homicide rate in many years, especially among youth. We need to ensure that people are safe in their own homes and that all neighborhoods are safe for young people, with access to quality education and opportunity. We need to completely rethink prisons, to enact sensible gun laws, and to treat drug addiction. And yet, for every person lost during the time of my ministry there were many more who triumphed over extremely difficult conditions, and many who continue to triumph bravely every day.

A final section of the book deals with my move to Pennsylvania to work with the Pendle Hill Quaker study center. I was charged with starting a program for youth in the nearby small post industrial city of Chester. The program served adjudicated youth, and once more I experienced both the beauty of young people and the tragedy of violence in low-income urban neighborhoods. I was privileged to live and work with Quakers. Later I moved into Philadelphia and became involved with a socially active Episcopal community, The Philadelphia Episcopal Cathedral. I tell of my involvement there in a food pantry and an anti-violence program which led me to do spiritual direction in a Pennsylvania prison. I tell the story of one remarkable man who is incarcerated.

The chapters are essentially in chronological order relative to the events of my ministry. But they are interspersed with thematic chapters, which sometimes include people or material that has not been introduced. In addition, some stories cover a longer time period, so again I reference people and events that have not been introduced. I try to clarify in such situations. In many places I have changed the names of the people involved in the stories.

This book does double duty. It is the story of people and events that I encountered in the city through my ministry work and the programs in which I was engaged. Therefore, it highlights the social issues that are involved, especially issues of poverty, violence, and justice. And it is also a spiritual memoir of my time in urban ministry and my own growth in faith. I tell these stories from the perspective of a Unitarian Universalist Christian. While I have been a Christian for many years, there have been times when I preferred other titles or descriptions. There was the "feminist universalist Jesian" period. There was a time that I talked about the Goddess a lot and annoyed the more conventional Christians around me. Sometimes I still often prefer "Jesus follower," especially when I hear Christians described on the news, where too often evangelical, fundamentalist, nationalist, right-wing, and Christian seem to be synonymous terms.

Sometimes people act as though it is strange to be a Unitarian Universalist and a Christian. I understand. When I became a UU many years ago I was almost militantly anti-Christian. I had encountered a few hardline fundamentalists in my young life and if they exemplified what was Christian then I was not. In Unitarian Universalism I found a vibrant humanist faith; I found people with a passion to explore and search freely and bravely for meaning and put their lives on the line for social justice and love. I was all in. No God or Jesus or Bible or anything like that required.

Slowly, however, I understood that my personal "search for meaning" was a search for God, that "transcending mystery and wonder" named in the UU Principles and Purposes. And slowly, other kinds of Christians and ways of being Christian appeared in my life. I was introduced to liberation theology by Professor Marie August Neal; I worked in faith development with my advisor, Professor James Fowler; I embarked on spiritual direction in the way of St. Ignatius of Loyola, founder of the Jesuit order of priests; and I was embraced on the frontlines of urban ministry work, often by Roman Catholics, who lived their faith in solidarity with poor and marginalized people.

I traveled from the childhood Jesus who taught me to love my neighbor, and also that God loved me; to the God of liberation theology; and to the Ignatian God who is every day creating us in a world of love. I became a Christian in heart, mind, and soul; a mystical Christian; a universalist Christian; a Christian as a matter of love.

Religion is comprised of symbols and myths—forms of which can say more, not less, than literal speech. Religious symbols can take us to the experience that they symbolize. They are mystagogic. The Christian story is the religious symbol that most deeply touches my spirit.

Because religious language is rooted in symbol, it can be very complicated to talk about. God language is affected by culture, family, politics, and one's personal experience and even, in Jim Fowler's analysis, developmental faith stage. (Fowler 1995) People often hear the word God and think that they know what another person is talking about, and yet they may be completely off base.

Some of the most helpful advice that I have discovered in talking about God comes from theologian Elizabeth A. Johnson. Johnson offers three ground rules for talking about God. The first ground rule is to recognize that God is simply beyond our comprehension. In Johnson's words God is "so far beyond the world, and so deeply in the world as to be literally incomprehensible." If we think that we know what God is and we can explain God, we're wrong. The second ground rule is that "no expression for God can be taken literally. None." God talk is not literal speech. These two ground rules lead to the third, which is that because no one name for God can explain this mystery, we need many names for God. God can be father or mother, higher power, deeper power, liberator, king, queen, Yah, savior, helper, friend, inter-breathing spirit of the universe and so on and so on. God talk is never literal! (Johnson 2007)

So, if we think we know what God is, we're wrong. If we think that we know what another person means when they talk about God, we're probably wrong. We need to be careful, creative, and open minded when talking about God.

My approach to this writing is influenced by my practice of Ignatian spirituality. For several years I have been in spiritual direction, and I am a spiritual director in this tradition, which is based on the Spiritual Exercises of St. Ignatius of Loyola, the founder of the Society of Jesus, the Jesuit order of priests. As a Christian UU, I have found this path remarkably compatible with Unitarian Universalism. Both emphasize reason, imagination, spiritual freedom, action in the world, and a foundation in love. Today the Exercises are used widely with people from various denominations, as my longtime Spiritual Director, George Drury SJ often said, "The Holy Spirit moves in freedom."

The Spiritual Exercises of St. Ignatius, the foundation for Ignatian spirituality, is a program of various kinds of prayer and study to be engaged on a thirty-day retreat—or over more than twenty weeks in daily life—including meeting with a spiritual director. The retreat is divided into four weeks; what's called a week is a theme rather than a length of time. The theme of the first week is the good nature of Creation, God's unconditional love, and in the face of that, the brokenness and disorder called sin. The second week, often the longest, includes the life and teaching of Jesus and learning to be a disciple, praying for the grace deeply to know, love, and follow him. The third week is about crucifixion and the fourth week focuses on resurrection. The Exercises are meant to provide a foundation for one's loving action in the world. The last prayer in the Spiritual Exercises is called the Contemplation to Attain Love, sometimes referred to as a contemplation on "learning to love as God loves." St. Ignatius states that love is better known by what one does than what one says. Spirituality is not separate from one's life in the world. People often describe Ignatian spirituality by saying that "God is in all things" and identify its followers as active contemplatives, or contemplative activists.

In the Exercises, St. Ignatius teaches many forms of prayer. One form that is particularly identified with Ignatian spirituality is imaginative contemplation. Rather than emptying one's mind—which is the goal of some forms of prayer known as contemplation—this form of prayer uses story and imagination as a way to enable the Spirit to teach and move, to bring one closer to God. One prays a Biblical story, for example, by seeing it in the imagination and bringing all of one's senses to bear on it. What does it look like? What are the sounds in the scene? What are people saying? What are the scents, the colors? What do things feel like to the touch? What is the taste of the wine and the bread?

One watches the story unfold, even participates in the story, and trusts the imagination, moved by the Spirit, for instruction. The prayer concludes with an imaginative conversation with someone in the story, usually Jesus. Following the prayer, the person takes time to reflect on it, often journaling, to discern what insight or truth might have been experienced. It is a creative process. St. Ignatius counsels us to use all our faculties in approaching prayer and spiritual understanding: reason, experience, imagination, desire, knowledge, and free will.

In framing the stories of this book, I sometimes use quotations from the Bible to set the theme, but often I use creatively imagined Bible stories in this way, particularly stories of Jesus and his disciples. These Jesus stories can be seen as paradigms for human life lived in relation to the Sacred. I cite the stories that these imagined scenarios come from. Sometimes the stories include considerable material from my own imagining, sometimes they are closer to the story as simply presented in the New Testament. Through biblical imagery they reflect my theological perspective that all people are beloved children of God, each human person absolutely unique and important in the universe, each one a reflection of the Holy Mystery that we call God. God is within all things, and infinitely more than all things. God is unconditional love and seeks the wholeness of all in a world of justice, mercy, forgiveness, and peace. While I usually use the New Revised Standard Version of the Bible for quotations, I degenderize them.

Often as a clergywoman I would be asked to speak from a religious context. This might be at a gathering of young adolescents who had been involved in violent street gangs, or with women who had been abused by their partners and were seeking new lives. Sometimes I would be preaching or speaking to a congregation with many recovering drug addicts, or to a group wounded by what was once a true plague—AIDS. Or perhaps I would be speaking at an interfaith gathering of activists.

Always I would speak on some variation of the theological themes that are my faith and my hope. There is one God whose nature is absolute Love. This God may have many names, but there is one unified, whole, source of Being and this Holy Mystery is all love. And I would talk about the most important value to Unitarian Universalists as I understood it—the absolute worth and dignity of every human person. That included the gang member, the addict, the abused woman, even the abuser. Every person, absolutely.

It was an honor to serve in such a ministry at large, inspired by the history of the Rev. Dr. Joseph Tuckerman, supported by colleagues and friends in the community, and later by the warmth and vision of Friends (Quakers), especially at Pendle Hill in Pennsylvania, and the Episcopal community at St. Mary's Episcopal Church in Dorchester and the Philadelphia Episcopal Cathedral. In recent times I volunteered in a food pantry at the Cathedral. I participated in a noon liturgy followed by healing prayer with those recipients who so desired. I tried hard to learn people's names and circumstances and to act in a pastoral role. One day, I prayed briefly with Venus and as I tried to move on to the next person she held onto my hand. "Wait," she said. "I want to pray for you. Because it makes a difference that you are here." This is how I feel about all of the people in these stories. It makes a difference that they are, or have been, here.

BAPTISM

> I wish I could show you
> When you are lonely or in darkness
> The astonishing Light
> Of your own being.
>
> Hafiz, I Heard God Laughing: Poems of Hope and Joy

The Calling: A Journey into Ministry

Zacchaeus was doing pretty well for himself. He was chief tax collector and had a nice home, a steady income. True, many people hated him because he collaborated with the Roman Empire in their oppression and taxation of the people, but after all, what could he do about that? Might as well have a comfortable living. Recently he had been hearing about a wandering prophet in the land, quite a talented healer and preacher, people said. So, when he heard that this man, Jesus, was in town, he went to see. There was a big crowd and being short in stature Zacchaeus had to climb a tree to get a good view. Jesus saw him there and laughed, telling him to come down and invite him and his close followers to dinner! Zacchaeus was intrigued and so they all feasted that night at his house. There was something about Jesus that touched Zacchaeus, moved him in fact to make some generous financial gifts. Ultimately, the transformation that happened with this tax collector caused him to give up that collaboration with the oppressor forever and follow a new path, one inspired by the healer who saw him sitting in the tree. (Imagined from Luke 19:2)

It was a little white leather King James Bible, the one I received for my tenth birthday. My agnostic parents had been good enough and liberal enough to buy their daughter what she had asked for on her birthday. This strange phase would probably pass. They continued to give her fifty cents for the collection plate as she headed off up the hill on Sunday mornings on her way to church, and now they put up with it as she sat in the living room obviously reading the Bible in hopes of converting them.

I had not always been quite so enthusiastic about church. I'm told that during my first experience of Sunday School as a preschooler I stood up angrily and stomped out of the room. The teacher had read the Passover story in which a lamb is slaughtered, and I said that I wasn't going to have anything to do with a place that promoted killing baby animals. Nevertheless, later I attended church with my grandmother and loved it, apparently forgetting about the lamb, and as a child, became involved with a very compassionate and progressive United Methodist Church in Seattle where we lived. I learned all about Jesus and I heard and experienced that the message was love.

Sometimes I went to Sunday school, but usually I preferred to go to the church service. There I learned about people who were poor, who didn't have enough food or adequate homes. Usually, these people were in faraway lands. I learned that it was the Christian's responsibility to feed the hungry, clothe the naked, take in the homeless poor, and that there were people called missionaries who spent their lives doing this work. As a child this spoke directly to my heart, and I dreamed of being a missionary. I don't remember anything about missionaries being sent to convert people, just to help them. I had other fantasies about my future, I thought maybe I would be a minister's wife in a beautiful white church in the country like the picture on the church bulletin, (after all this was the 1950s.) But more seriously I remember asking my parents, my dad I think, could I be a minister? He said yes!

When I was twelve, I took a class with the minister in order to be baptized. I don't remember much except something about Methodists being methodical, and that I was required to memorize the 23rd Psalm, something for which I have long been grateful. My parents attended my baptism. My father was serving his monthly reserve Navy duty and came in his Commander's uniform. I was so proud.

My parents were right about my religious zeal diminishing, at least in the short term; my religious devotion lasted somewhat into my early teen years but did not survive a tumultuous high school experience. Some of this was normal faith development, as I later came to understand it. My childhood faith gave way to questioning, what had seemed real and true to the younger child did not seem logically real or true, and following and looking to Jesus Christ did not help me in the high school world of alcohol, sex, and rock and roll. One night, as an intoxicated, devastated teenager, left alone in my front yard by friends, I actually turned to the heavens and shouted angrily at God, "I do not believe in you. Go away. Just leave me alone! "I became almost hostile to organized religion.

Existentialism, Zen Buddhism, and Art as God dominated my college years. While I continued not to believe in something called "God" I maintained a longing for something beyond, something real and transcendent, my old Christian God of universal love. One day, for example, I was sitting in the local coffee shop reading a book that someone had recommended by Nikolai Berdyaev, a Christian existentialist. Berdyaev emphasized creativity and personal existential freedom while being rooted in Christian theology. I was so excited reading this that the waitress came over and asked me if I was all right! The idea of an existentialist Christian, an existentialist who held out the possibility of God, was breathtaking to me. Nevertheless, I clung rather to Sartre, who said something to the effect that existentialists did not believe in God, but they cared more about God than most believers.

I was a theatre major and sometimes experienced a kind of transcendence in giving myself over to the character, being part of the whole production, part of something larger than myself and of greater value. Art. Today I consider this a true spiritual vocation, part of my search for God. I believed this with my whole heart. One of my mentors was a young artist, Mel Hanson, who often declared that art demanded one's whole attention and being. Mel was a talented painter whom I met when he was promoting a party called Japonica at his studio. He was riding around campus in his open jeep yelling Ja-PON-ica. Japonica is a Japanese plant, but Mel liked the name and declared its true meaning to be Curly of the Three Stooges and Marilyn Monroe in passionate embrace.

I went to the Japonica party and became sweethearts and then close friends with this charming, challenging, inspiring artist. We were friends for almost three years, Mel critiqued my acting and inspired me with his passion. He believed that we should give all we had to our art and seek greatness. "I may make mistakes," he said, "but they'll be great mistakes!" One night, mailing a letter, Mel ran across the street in front of a car and was thrown 30 feet. I was with him the next day in the hospital when he died. It was a Saturday and I had gone to lunch in the college dining hall when someone approached me and told me that Mel had been critically wounded. I struggled with what that meant and found a friend to drive me to the hospital. I spent several hours there with Mel's mother and with Mel who was unconscious and hooked up to a variety of machines. At one point I stood by his side, telling him how I felt about him and listening to the sound of his breathing through the tube in his neck, and all of a sudden, the sound stopped. The doctors came running but they could not revive him.

I left the hospital and went straight to the theatre where I had to perform as Rosalind in Shakespeare's *As You Like It.* My wonderful director, DeMarcus Brown, had me run through a couple of scenes first to make sure I could do it. I tried to lift my soul to a spiritual realm, to do this for Mel, to do this for Art. I got through it, but I felt no spirit. No transcendence. I felt nothing but stunned, numb, horrified. Dead. Mel was dead. Melvin Charles Hanson was dead. How could this brilliant, gifted friend whom I loved die? This Artist!? Where was God? What was God? Another pure and simple absence.

A year later I gave up my theatre career when I met, fell in love with, and married Herb Adams, in spite of the fact that he was a minister. Unitarian Universalism was different, he said. And it was, and God began to call me back through this generous humanistic religion which offered me the free and responsible search for meaning - and we didn't have to deal with that disappointing, abandoning, incomprehensible, or even silly God. At first my attraction was to the social witness and action of the denomination during the civil rights movement of the sixties, and then involvement in the protest against the U.S. war in Vietnam. In those years my life was graced with two great loves, children, a boy named Lee and a girl named Rachel. They became the center of my world which, along with my continuing, if qualified, interest in religion led me to become a Unitarian Universalist religious educator. I worked first part time at the Follen Church in Lexington, Massachusetts where I studied and became certified, and then full time at the First Parish in Lexington. Those years included not just the joy of family, the companionship of a partner, but also the sadness of misunderstanding, separation, and divorce. I became a single mother, working, parenting, and trying to find meaning.

I defined religion according to the root word, *relegare,* to hold together. And faith as a verb. And God in a variety of Tillichian (Paul Tillich) phrases, "the ground of being," "the source of ultimate concern," "God beyond God." I loved religious education at that time and remember being involved in summer conferences at Star Island, a conference center off the coast of New Hampshire. One summer I designed and led a workshop named Doing Your Own Theology. I don't remember much about it except that it included a good amount of Bob Dylan, Leonard Cohen, and Joan Baez.

My children grew and I became restless in my vocation as religious educator, and began to look to other possibilities, including becoming a psychotherapist. I brought my concerns to my colleague, Senior Minister of the First Church, Bob Zoerheide, who said instantly and enthusiastically, "the ministry, Betty, the ministry!" And I knew as he said it, yes, yes, the ministry. Of course. The Unitarian Universalist ministry. There was a sense of clarity and rightness about this path.

And so, with the help of the UUA Department of ministry, I was accepted into an Independent Study Program with most of my course work to happen at Harvard Divinity School. As a religious educator I had worked with James Fowler, a young professor there who was developing a theory of faith development along the lines of Lawrence Kohlberg's moral development. I was a research assistant one year for Jim, interviewing young children, and I had been excited to celebrate with him at the Harvard Faculty Club on the occasion of his first large grant. Jim graciously agreed to be my advisor in the Independent Study Program.

The first class that Jim recommended was The Sociology of Religion taught by Marie August Neal, SND deN. a hugely consequential recommendation. This class became a critically important event in my faith and ministry life. After covering various sociologists of religion and culture and asking us continually to react to their thinking in relation to our conception of God (what was my conception of God—did I even have one?) she introduced liberation theology which at that time, in the 1970s, was emerging as a powerful force for justice, especially in Latin America. Liberation theologians declared that God is on the side of the oppressed and marginalized and seeks their liberation—real liberation from economic want and hardship. God takes a "preferential option for the poor" the Latin American bishops pronounced. This moved me deeply and I understood that this was the ministry to which I was called, to minister in solidarity with the marginalized and poor who were seeking freedom.

When Bob suggested that I pursue the UU ministry I had a sense of rightness and clarity! Yes, the ministry. When I learned of liberation theology, I felt a sense of depth and excitement which moved beyond that clarity into passion. This was my calling at this time in my life. Not to minister in a church, a vocation which I understood well having worked in UU churches for nine years, but somehow to be with people in community sharing in the struggle for freedom and justice.

As Illia Delio said in her memoir, "A religious vocation is not like a job application or a personal assessment. It is an unmerited, pure gift of grace. It is a 'call,' because the grace of God awakens within unannounced, like a high-pitched alarm clock...blaring when you least expect it. It is an invasion, an interruption if not outright intrusion of grace, and it does not allow you to go back to the rest of your former life without either forgetting what you heard or responding to the gift." (Delio 2019).

This was the ministry to which I was called. But how or where? I met with Dr. Neal, and she was happy to hear that I was intending to go into the Unitarian Universalist ministry, understanding that this was an affluent, largely white denomination. "Good," she said, "when the people come for what is rightfully theirs there must be people to teach the haves to let go." I understood the truth of this sentence, there must be leaders and educators who teach and preach justice and structural change to the "haves" of our society. Nevertheless, while I appreciated Dr. Neal's words, this did not speak to my heart, rather her words one day in class "People go to the country to find God because God is too hard to take in the city." While I understood that I had experienced a true call to community justice seeking ministry, I had no idea how I would answer that call.

The second major recommendation from Jim had to do with Ignatian spiritual direction. Spiritual direction is a discipline in which the director listens to the directee talk about their spiritual life, their relationship with God, or questions of ultimate meaning, and gives them help or suggestions regarding prayer and or related disciplines. Ignatian Spiritual direction is based on the Spiritual Exercises of St. Ignatius. I didn't have a comfortable language for God or a regular spiritual practice, and therefore it was difficult for me to continue to grow in faith. Jim recommended the Jesuit center in Cambridge, and although the Center's regular directors were not accepting new people, they referred me to Father Lou Lipps SJ, who was in Cambridge for a few months and open to seeing people for spiritual direction.

Father Lou was staying in a parish rectory in East Cambridge. I remember entering the very Roman Catholic building with its dark wood and crucifixes. This was foreign territory to me. All of my liberal church experience had been in very light buildings with lots of windows and few symbols – UUs of course generally had no symbols (a symbol in itself) and my childhood Methodist church had little but an empty cross. There was a medieval feeling to that rectory in East

Cambridge, and that was strangely appealing.

Ft. Lou had a long red beard and black clergy clothes, and welcomed me warmly. He heard that I had no experience with prayer and gave me some initial suggestions, including the recommendation that I pray with some particular psalms, and explained how to do that. Read the psalm slowly, if a word or phrase moves you, stay with it, skip over lines that do not speak to you. Let the psalm be a way of speaking to God, and perhaps hearing God speak to you.

Lou knew that I was UU and was careful about language and theology, but still I found it hard to talk about "God" as some sort of relational personal presence. My conception of God by that time had to do with a just and loving spiritual force underlying all being - but doesn't prayer imply a Person!? Talk to God? Who are you talking to?! In fact, my underlying understanding of God as G-O-D was, while largely internalized and unconscious, still a big patriarchal male being. A Person, as we are persons—the framed, limited, hierarchical idea of modern theism. I had no inclination at all to talk to that! On the other hand, how do you talk to the "source of ultimate concern" or the "ground of being?"

At that point, I was in the second year of my study program, and I was feeling both restless and called, and very stressed and perhaps depressed. I had finished therapy after two years (and I think that my insurance had run out) but felt good about the experience except that I had not quit smoking which was one of the reasons I had started therapy. So, I decided I would quit and went to a behavioral program. That was very bad timing for I was already feeling on complete overload with work, parenting, and study—and doing it alone. Sadly, my marriage with Herb had not survived tumultuous years and changes, and Herb had taken a job in Chicago and moved there with our son, Lee. The loss of Lee's nearby presence added a layer of grief to the stress that I was feeling.

So, during this period I decided to suspend my disbelief in a personal God, and my discomfort, and try to learn to pray, to see if I could somehow experience some kind of relational "God." I was surprised. Right away as I prayed the psalms in the way that Lou had suggested I began to hear God, whatever that was, speak to me through the prayer and scripture. But I was still feeling barely able to cope with my super-scheduled life, and I am sure I was also terrified underneath it all, that I just could not achieve the goals I had set. After only one or two spiritual direction sessions I had a day in which I simply couldn't handle the pressure of it all anymore. I imploded. I had scheduled one morning to read a "little" book by Alfred North Whitehead for a class on Religious Experience. And I couldn't do it. I kept reading the first page over and over. I couldn't get through a single paragraph without my mind wandering, and of course the more I tried the more desperate and distracted I felt.

At one point I got up for something and saw myself in a mirror as I was passing by. Seeing myself, I was, in an instant, gripped by an overwhelming rage. Without thinking, I hurled a wooden clog at my image in the mirror—at that horribly stupid and inadequate person I saw reflected, who couldn't even read a simple damn book!

The mirror shattered. It was a large mirror attached to a dresser that I had had since I was first married. I walked over to it to look at the damage and all of the little pieces held a reflection of me. There seemed to be hundreds of that loathsome person staring back. I reacted violently. I thought fiercely that I had to hurt myself, and I headed down to the kitchen to get a knife, but I had only taken a couple of steps before I realized that my daughter, Rachel, would come home from school and find me. The violent rage instantly vanished and I sat down on the stairs and wept, before cleaning up the mess. I was frightened and despairing at my self-destructive rage, horrified that I would do anything that might hurt Rachel so terribly, and her brother, Lee as well. That night I drank much too much red wine and was physically sick the next day, unable to take Rachel to a church fair. I felt sorry about that. But I was alive. She and Lee still had a mother!

I took this to Lou with deep shame. My destructive rage in breaking the mirror was bad enough, but to have even a brief moment of suicidal intention was almost unspeakable. I loved my children more than anything in my life. How could I have reacted in a way that would cause so much pain.

I looked at Lou whose face took on such a look of compassion, "oh, thank God for your children!!!!" he said. I was stunned. It was not what I expected. I expected him to agree with me about how awful I was and tell me to seek forgiveness. But his reaction instead was to be grateful—grateful that I was alive, thanking God for my children because they kept me alive. Thankful that love kept me alive.

This was one of those transforming moments that are so hard to describe. I judged myself harshly and I expected to be judged in that way, rather than to be met with compassion, and even gratitude that I was alive. Lou, the priest, cared that I was alive—not because he needed me in any way personally, or others needed me, but just because I was. Me.

And I knew, though not in a way I could articulate at the time, that the Spirit was loving me through Lou Lipps. God had led me to him at a time when I was delicately balanced and searching, stretched almost beyond my capacity, and God loved and cherished me and was constantly present to me, even though I was not aware. It was a moment in which I understood, at a level beyond words, that love had conquered death—for myself and for my children. And God, always beyond real definition, became personal for me—not a person, but truly personal.

That began many years of Ignatian spiritual direction for me, a spirituality rooted in God's steadfast love and constant presence in relationship—relationship with God, with other human beings in a life of love; relationship within the self where God's spirit and other spirits can be known; a spirituality of forgiveness and mercy; in which God creates us "momently," in which every life is sacred simply because it exists in God's greater love and intention. I was enormously graced through the years of urban ministry to be in spiritual direction with two amazing directors, George Drury SJ for many years in Boston, and John Kerdiejus SJ who directed my thirty-day retreat of the Spiritual Exercises of St. Ignatius.

Lou was only in town for a short time, although he was there a year later at the time of my ordination. He attended and participated in the laying on of hands. I treasure that (and consider myself to be partially Jesuit!).

The encounter with liberation theology, Ignatian spirituality, and my earlier experience with faith development led me gradually along a faith path that was increasingly Christian. Understanding faith development, those earlier experiences of Jesus and the scriptures laid a foundation that could speak to me in a deeper, more complex and mature manner as I got older; and through liberation theology I saw Jesus as the Jewish peasant who was crucified by the state for his powerful love, advocacy, and presence with the poor and oppressed; the resurrection turning the violence and death into life and hope. Finally, Ignatian spirituality led me into a conscious relationship with the Holy Mystery we call God, and a follower in the symbolic way of Jesus. My Christian life unfolded over time, and still unfolds as God creates us "momently."

I completed my training in 1978 and went before the ministerial fellowship committee of the UUA, the credentialing body for clergy. Our meeting had an awkward beginning. The male president of the committee started by telling me that I was better looking than my picture. I was quite taken aback, wondering how I should respond to what seemed like a sexist remark. Should I challenge the chair of the committee which had the power to credential me for UU ministry? Was my integrity or my future on the line here? Seeing my reaction, a woman sitting next to me, one of the few female ministers at that time, hastily showed me the picture that was included in the packet. In it my face was totally blurred and unrecognizable. I said "Oh," laughed, and we got on with what was a good interview. I explained that I hoped to work in community in solidarity with people on the margins, and they wished me well, approving me for Unitarian Universalist parish ministry.

The classes, the internship, Clinical Pastoral Education, and now the MFC review and approval—it was all finished. Soon I would be ordained, ready to begin this new ministry. But what exactly was that ministry?! What would I do? Community-based ministries with people seeking liberation and justice were hardly advertised. I had come to believe, however, that this was a true calling, rooted in my growing understanding and relationship with Holy Mystery and that, as Quakers say, "way would open."

I had been active during those years in supporting the United Farm Workers (UFW) union boycotts and had become friendly with a UFW organizer. He told me that the National Council of Churches (NCC) had a farmworkers ministry out in California, and that I should look into it. I contacted the head of the ministry, the Rev. Chris Hartmire, and he suggested that we talk. I was planning to visit my parents in Northern California and so I arranged to meet Chris at the UFW headquarters in the hills outside of LA. This was an old tuberculosis hospital which had become La Paz, the headquarters for the UFW. There I met with some of the religious people working for the union, had a meal with a former priest and nun, now married. I was excited to meet Cesar Chavez himself who warmly welcomed me on hearing that I was considering the farmworker ministry. Chris offered me a position with the NCC ministry, living in a communal house farther north in the valley, helping the union with contract negotiations with farmers, and speaking at churches and other gatherings about the issues concerning farmworkers to organize support for the union's activities.

This was very exciting to me. Rachel and I would live in a house with other organizers and while I would be paid minimally, Chris said there would be other funds to see that son Lee, living with his father in Chicago, could go back and forth. And I would be near my parents as they aged. It certainly fit the liberation theology agenda that I was seeking. I would live and work with people who were struggling for freedom and justice. I returned to Massachusetts to prepare for ordination, with the expectation of returning in the following months to California.

A ministry with the National Council of Churches farmworker ministry would certainly have been a meaningful ministry, but I was in for a surprise as my life took another turn. I attended a local weekend conference of Unitarian Universalists and signed up for whatever workshop sounded most interesting, undoubtedly something having to do with social justice. As we introduced ourselves, I expressed my desire to work in a community-based social justice ministry, and as we went around the room it was clear that I had sparked an interest in a young, tall, bearded, minister. He introduced himself as Scotty McLennan, doing what he called a ministry at large for the Benevolent Fraternity of Unitarian Churches. I couldn't imagine what that was. He said he was a lawyer and minister and was attempting to combine these things in what he called a legal ministry in poor communities. I was excited by his vision, but Benevolent Fraternity of Unitarian Churches? What was a Benevolent Fraternity? An association of kindly old Unitarian guys?

Scotty and I talked after the workshop and he told me about the Benevolent Fraternity, nicked named Ben Frat, which was an old Unitarian agency founded in 1834 to provide ministers at large, ministers outside of specific churches, in low-income communities of the city. The ministers at large created their ministries based on the specifics and needs of the community, but the mission was to provide liberating ministry to people who were poor in the city. He said that there was some discussion at the agency of hiring a woman minister to create some form of ministry with women. He urged me to call the Executive director, Reverend Bud (Virgil) Murdock.

I met with Bud and learned that another old Boston nonprofit, this time Universalist, The Franklin Square House, was seeking to partner with the Ben Frat to create a joint ministry. The Franklin Square House's mission was to provide safe, supportive housing to women in the city, but its mission of supervised housing was no longer relevant to the times, so it was seeking to provide another form of housing service to women. It would provide space for a program supervised by the Ben Frat. I met with various people to get ideas on how such a housing space could be used. One suggestion was to create a shelter for women who were being abused and were fleeing violence. This was early in the days when domestic violence was being recognized as a problem and women were organizing to create shelters to help other women to be safe. As I looked into this, I became more and more excited by the idea and proposed such a shelter to Bud. The idea was accepted by both boards of directors and after a wonderful, life affirming ordination by the First Parish in Lexington I accepted the call to be associate minister at large at the Benevolent Fraternity of Unitarian Churches. I was sad not to pursue the ministry with the UFW, and especially sad not to live closer to my parents, but the idea of a UU ministry in poor communities in the city, with women, felt like a clear call to me.

I had traveled an ever-deepening spiritual path from that church on the hill in Seattle and my desire to be minister and missionary. Now I found myself not a missionary as Ben Frat's founder made clear, nor a Unitarian Universalist parish minister, but a minister at large, joyfully in the tradition of many who preceded me. My path would continue to deepen and transform as I entered into relationships with countless beautiful people through the years. Truly, the adventure, the spiritual journey was just beginning as I moved into the city of Boston in August of 1978.

Zacchaeus was like so many people that Jesus encountered. It had not been possible for him simply to meet Jesus and then go on his way. Like that woman with the hemorrhage, the man possessed by multiple demons, the Samaritan woman at the well, the man born blind from birth, like these and many others he found Jesus's message transforming inside and out. He could not go backward but had to make a change. He didn't know where he was going, or exactly what he would do, but he knew that it would be a journey well worth taking. (Imagined from Mark 5:1-34; John 4:1-26; John 9:1-7)

Joseph Tuckerman and the Ministry at Large

Simon Peter and his brother, Andrew, and the brothers Zebedee had been at work all morning, fishing. It was hard work but work that they were used to. They knew how to make nets, mend nets, and take care of the fishing boats. They knew when and where fish were likely to be. They were pretty good at catching them in a steady way – nothing spectacular, but it was good work, they understood it.

While they were content in their work, however, the general political situation of the country, struggling under the Roman Empire's rules and taxation, left them in a larger and deeper way discontented with their lives, restless for something better. And then one day a man named Jesus appeared. They knew Jesus a little bit, he had grown up in the next town, and there had been occasions to meet him. He was a bit eccentric, but interesting and rather appealing. Nevertheless, it was astonishing that when he stopped by their boats and asked them to leave everything and follow him, they did so immediately. How could they do something so rash! What would they find if they left the comfort of what they knew and accepted his invitation? "Come, follow me," he had said to them, I will make you fish for people." (Imagined from Mark 1:7-8)

The story of the UU Urban Ministry goes back to 1826. In those days, the Reverend Joseph Tuckerman met often with his good friend the Reverend William Ellery Channing at the Federal Street Church in Boston. Channing was a prominent leader in the Unitarian movement of the early 19th century, from which came the Unitarian church, and later the Unitarian Universalist denomination. Defining important concepts of the movement in a sermon in Baltimore called "Unitarian Christianity," Channing helped to lay the foundation for the new denomination. He and Tuckerman had been friends since their youth and had attended Harvard together.

The two old friends talked of many things, but a common subject was the growing poverty in Boston. Tuckerman wanted to know more about the life of those who were poor in the city. This was a different kind of poverty than he had seen before, different from the occasional times of hardship in the rural parish in which he ministered. In the country, when weather or other conditions caused crops to fail and there was a hard time in the community, people would gather and share what they had. People all knew one another and rallied around to help.

In large parts of the city, it was different. There were growing neighborhoods, spawned by factories, where large numbers of people had moved from the country to find work, and were crowded together. These held not the beautiful brick townhouses of Beacon Hill where he had grown up, or the elegant farmhouses of Roxbury and Dorchester. These neighborhoods were filled with poorly made wooden or stone structures into which large families were jammed on top of one another. Tuckerman was concerned about these communities where the factory workers lived and where their children often roamed the streets, unattended and often hostile. He had seen the poorly clad of these neighborhoods. He was distressed that people lived in such conditions and he wanted to know more. Why were they living in such crowded and dilapidated conditions? What was the cause of this poverty? What were their lives like? What did they feel and believe? What help did they need?

As a Unitarian Christian minister, Tuckerman's life was centered around Jesus and his teaching to love God and to love one's neighbor as oneself. He attempted to listen to the voice of God through Christ, and to follow the call of God where he discerned it. He believed that God's love was for all the people, each made in God's image and that each should have equal opportunity. Tuckerman believed that good-willed people could solve social problems and create a just society for everyone. He asked himself why the lives of these people were seemingly so desperate. And what could others do to help?

Tuckerman was a practical man and figured that the easiest way to know something about someone was to ask them. So, the Reverend Tuckerman went door to door in the poor neighborhoods of Boston, introducing himself to the residents, sitting down with them, getting to know them, asking about their lives, offering a prayer or a blessing if asked. He kept careful records, making notes after visiting each home. What he learned filled him with energy and conviction and, most importantly, with a new and powerful call in ministry. He would be a minister to the poor of the city! Tuckerman resigned from his rural parish in Chelsea, Massachusetts and, with Channing's help and support, jumped right into his new ministry.

At first Tuckerman considered himself a missionary. "I will be a missionary to the poor," he thought, and he was overjoyed for he had always wanted to enter the mission field. He continued going door to door to ascertain what he could do to minister to the needs of the people. However, before long he stopped calling himself a missionary. This was a ministry like all ministries, he realized; it simply did not exist within a church building. All of the offices of ministry were needed: the pastoral, the priestly, the religious educator, the preacher, the prophet, the administrator. Tuckerman considered the prophetic calling especially important as he brought the reality of poor communities into the privileged world of greater Boston. He announced that he would now be called not a missionary, but a minister at large. Soon Tuckerman and Channing had involved many others and the funds were raised to hire several ministers at large.

Through the years the Rev. Tuckerman was engaged in many dimensions of the battle against urban poverty, addressing issues of poor working conditions, poor wages, unjust treatment of women, terrible housing conditions, lack of educational facilities, mental health issues, substance abuse, juvenile crime, and the justice system in general. He said that he would "as soon send a sick person to a place where people had the plague to get well as he would send a youth to a prison." While he wrote and spoke on issues of poverty, Tuckerman and his colleagues also established chapels for religious education and worship, and a variety of outreach programs to help people in the community.

Tuckerman considered himself as a pastor and priest with the people in the low income neigborhoods where he worked. He declared that he saw the face of Jesus in everyone he met and loved ministering with the many people that he met in poor neighborhoods. At the same time he believed that the ministry at large was also called to educate the affluent about their involvement in the continuation of urban poverty. He believed that it was the moral and religious responsibility of the whole community to eliminate poverty. Therefore, he understood his ministry as serving both the rich and poor.

The Benevolent Fraternity of Unitarian Churches (later nicknamed the Ben Frat, and more recently doing business as the UU Urban Ministry) was organized in 1834 to continue the ministry at large. Through the years, programs changed, neighborhoods changed, and the Ben Frat continued to try to respond to the needs of the time and place, seeking to serve people who were poor in the city through the ministry at large, in different ways at different times.

It seemed like a crazy thing to do, perhaps, but Simon and Andrew and John and James left their fishing boats and followed Jesus. They traveled up and down the land and witnessed extraordinary events as this teacher, Jesus, healed and fed multitudes, preached amazing sermons on love and forgiveness and mercy. They met wonderful people in a surprisingly equalitarian setting, as Jesus welcomed all manner of people into the community. Sadly, they were also to witness oppression, hunger, violence and a range of suffering, most of it unnecessary, but imposed on the people by an Empire and its unjust reign. However, they gradually came to understand that, following Jesus, they were witnessing an alternative reign, a reign of justice and love being born among them, and for which they were called to be responsible.

Just Don't Walk Down St. Alphonsus Street

When Jesus of Nazareth traveled to the Jordan River to see his cousin John, who was baptizing people there, he caused quite a stir. John insisted that Jesus, too, be baptized, and it was rumored that when Jesus emerged from the water a dove flew down and landed on him! Someone was heard to refer to Jesus as the Spirit of God…or strangely, the lamb of God! What could that mean? Jesus was just an ordinary guy from Nazareth, what was all the fuss about? Two of John's disciples were curious about that and decided to follow him and see what was so special about him. Jesus noticed that he was being followed, and he turned around to question the two people. "What are you looking for?" he asked. "Where are you staying?" they asked in return. And then Jesus invited them simply to come and see. (Imagined from John 1:35–39)

In August of 1978 I moved with my eleven-year-old daughter, Rachel, and my shaggy dog, Chouchou, into the Mission Hill section of Boston to begin a ministry in the tradition of Joseph Tuckerman's ministry at large. I could not believe my good fortune in being called to this ministry, hired to do exactly what I had dreamed of doing: a community-based ministry in the style of liberation theology, in solidarity with those struggling for freedom and wholeness.

Rachel and I set out to discover our Mission Hill neighborhood, a vibrant and very diverse place. On one side was the Brigham and Women's Hospital complex, and within walking distance were the Museum of Fine Arts, Harvard Medical School, and the Fenway. The hill itself, named Parker Hill, was filled with traditional Boston working-class housing: triple-deckers, where three generations of the same family often lived. Mission Hill was originally predominately Irish, now a mix of families and singles, racially and economically diverse. That neighborhood was dominated by Our Lady of Perpetual Help, Boston's huge Catholic basilica. To the side and behind the basilica was the Mission Hill low-rise public housing development, and further down the street stood the Mission Hill high-rise low-income housing projects.

I began to notice a familiar refrain as I talked with people about the neighborhood, especially white people. "It's a nice neighborhood," they would say, "just don't walk down St. Alphonsus Street." I was reminded of the Peter Rabbit story that my mother read to me as a child. As I remembered it, a certain refrain was repeated in one part of the story, and my sister and I used to chant it, it went something like: "Yes, you may go out to play, just don't go into Farmer McGregor's garden."

Of course, Peter Rabbit does, losing his clothes in the process. "Yes, you may go out to play," people seemed to be saying, "just don't go down St. Alphonsus Street."

Of course, I went down St. Alphonsus Street and what did I discover? There were conventional private high-rise apartment buildings on one side; on the other side stood several blocks of public housing known as the Mission Main housing projects, which were what the white people of the neighborhood had warned against. But what was so scary about the housing projects? Who lived there that made it so threatening? As I came to know the neighborhood, I discovered that this "scary" area was filled with women and children. Babies. Mothers and fathers. Grandmothers. Little boys and girls, playing. Who lives in low-income housing developments like these in cities? Families.

The residents of Mission Main were largely Latino and African American. So, was I to understand that it was okay for low-income women and children of color to live there, but as white people, my children and I should not walk down the street next to it?

Naturally there were some practical aspects to the advice. There had been a rash of purse snatchings by teenagers from the development, who disappeared into the projects. One has to pay attention on city streets, and certainly there are times and places when certain streets can be dangerous to some who would walk down them. But there was a mythic quality to the situation that I found startling. People were separated into different streets and neighborhoods, keeping their daily lives out of sight and out of mind, making them seem, unconsciously perhaps, essentially different. And what was different became dangerous. Women and children. Families.

The power of this mythology was evident many years later when St. Alphonsus Street was the site of a big news story. Charles Stuart, a white man, shot his pregnant wife to death in his car while parked on St. Alphonsus Street, then wounded himself, claiming that they had been shot by a black man who then ran into Mission Main. The police initially believed the story and turned the projects upside down looking for the shooter. They arrested an unfortunate man who happened to fit the fabricated description. The public was quite ready to believe the story and it was some time before the truth came out, only because of the testimony of Stuart's brother, who had gotten rid of the gun. The power of the myth of our essential difference, enhanced by our separation from one another, made Stuart's story believable to the police and the public and almost cost an innocent man his freedom. While this was a major news story in Boston, the underlying racism causes similar injustices regularly in our cities.

There was no wicked Farmer McGregor here in my neighborhood, looking to make "rabbit stew." There were families doing the best they could to raise their children, but facing the obstacles of racism, poverty, an illegal drug industry, a proliferation of guns, and various forms of violence.

Before moving into Mission Hill I lived in a suburb of Boston where I worked as a Director of Religious Education. One of my volunteer teachers often drove into Boston to get materials at a discount store in Roxbury, the neighborhood where Mission Hill was located. Roxbury has many African American residents and is generally thought of as a black community. I was surprised that this woman would go there for supplies and wondered whether it was safe.

Because there was so much negative press about Roxbury, especially after the forced busing traumas of the 1970s, I had internalized the idea that this black community was somehow not safe for white people to travel into—a foreign land. This social mythology—this lie—is built into our whole way of thinking. It robs us of the truth and damages our wholeness as human beings, all of us. And for people of color and people who are poor, it deprives them of the full range of freedoms that others in our society enjoy. I often tried to make this point in sermons at many of our supporting Unitarian Universalist churches: we are all human together, we all suffer joys, and we all have our losses, our pain, our wounds. But it's easier to cope with the losses and pain when our home is secure and we have plenty of food; when we know that no one will turn us away based on our race or economic status; when we believe that social institutions such as the police and the courts are there to protect us, not to endanger us. We all suffer from time to time. Some people have constant additional burdens due to the racism that underlies our understanding of reality.

I came to love this diverse neighborhood, eventually moving into the third floor of one of those triple-deckers with Rachel and my son, Lee, who had been living with his father. Our dog was now joined by a cat who had belonged to one of the shelter residents who was unable to keep her when she moved. Later I moved to Uphams Corner in Dorchester, another vibrant, diverse community of amazing people with whom to work and love and struggle for peace and justice, laughter, and opportunity.

The disciples followed Jesus to see where he was staying. And they were surprised to see him hanging out with people in the "projects." He was playing with the children, sharing in the cookout, listening to the music, and just fully enjoying his time behind the great big basilica. Jesus liked being there in the shadow of Our Lady of Perpetual Help; he especially liked being with so many wonderful people.

You Are the Beloved—All of You

His first thirty years had not been easy. He had tried to work hard and fit in but so often he felt called away from that conventional life and found himself out of sync with his family and culture. Sometimes people even accused him of being possessed or out of his mind. Always, however, there was his cousin John who understood and would listen to him. John, in fact, was considered a bit crazy himself. Nevertheless, the two of them shared a vision of a world that was transformed, a world in which God's holy commandments were taken seriously, to love God and to love one's neighbor with all of one's heart, soul, and life instead of paying honor to the Empire and all who served it.

Jesus felt that he needed to see John, who had moved out into the wilderness near the Jordan River and was preaching and calling people to repentance. So, he traveled south to find his cousin and found him in the midst of baptizing countless people in the river. They spent the night together and John suggested that Jesus too have that experience of cleansing, repenting, of being washed clean in the holy waters. Jesus agreed and the next day he went with his lifelong friend, his loving cousin, into the Jordan River and was baptized there. Jesus went under the cool water of the river and when he came up out of the water something amazing happened. The sky opened up and a dove flew down to Jesus, landing on his hand. Jesus heard a voice, resounding around him, "This is my child, the beloved." (Imagined from Luke 3:21–22)

When I initially interviewed for a position at the Benevolent Fraternity, I had proposed to them that the space that the Franklin Square House was willing to donate to benefit women in need be used as a confidential shelter for women who were being abused. In those years, the late 1970s, society was becoming aware of the plight of women who were trapped in violent relationships, with nowhere to go and no one to help. They had accepted my proposal and the then Benevolent Fraternity had called me as an associate minister at large to create a shelter for what were then called "battered women" in the space offered by Franklin Square House.

Rachel and I had moved to be near the donated space, which consisted of three bedrooms, an office space, a tiny kitchen, and bathroom with no shower. (The space was later expanded on two different occasions.) The Franklin Sq. House director had said that it would be cleaned, but that meant only a very minimal cleaning. There were some beds and dressers placed in the space from the old Franklin Square House housing for women.

Of course, I did not expect to run a shelter by myself and saw that my primary activity needed to be networking within the community to build support and involvement. In the meantime, however, the space might be used briefly in emergencies that did not require staff support. But the place was a mess. Eleven-year-old Rachel and I decided to take on the task of readying the place, cleaning it and using the few donated items that had come in as churches heard of the effort. My old parish in Lexington supplied us with blankets and sheets. When we decided that we were ready to open, Rachel thought that the rooms needed brightening and brought over some little jars filled with flowers, putting one on each dresser to add something cheerful.

Although it would be a little time before we began operations, thanks to Rachel's help, the space was ready.

During this first year of the ministry at large, I volunteered at an established bilingual shelter for women who were victims of domestic violence, Casa Myrna. I wanted to learn all that I could about the experience of women in crisis and how to help them; learn about creating and running a shelter; and develop relationships with people doing this work. I became close to staff members there who shared my vision of creating another shelter for women in crisis, using space offered by the Franklin Square House. We agreed to use this space, temporarily, as overflow for Casa Myrna, accepting only women who could live there without full-time resident staff.

In addition to the overflow intakes from Casa Myrna, I began to take in women from trusted sources in my community, especially from Suzanne, a social worker who was a tireless advocate and presence for her clients. She would continue to act as an advocate for women whom I accepted as residents, or "guests," of what I had begun to call the Franklin Square Ministry (FSM).

One day I saw Suzanne on the subway. She did not see me because she was so involved in reading a book, the title of which I could see clearly, and which included the words, The Radical Social Worker. That was Suzanne, who would speak truth to power about the abuse of vulnerable and poor people, advocate for change, and try to move heaven and earth for each client. Suzanne understood that our limited shelter space, without resident or full-time staff, could only accept women who could safely live unsupervised. She recommended Laura as a guest of the new shelter.

Laura was a beautiful young woman who was recovering from serious brain damage. She had been pushed out of a third-story window by her drug-dealer boyfriend. After being in rehab for more than a year, it was determined that she was able to live on her own but given her obvious limitations she was having trouble finding an apartment. Laura walked slowly with a cane and had difficulty speaking, but her thinking was clear, and she was fiercely determined to recover and be independent. Suzanne was equally fierce in her determination to find Laura a home.

Laura was not the first resident of the FSM, but she was the first to stay more than a day or two. She enjoyed the freedom and independence that having her own place gave her and made good use of this time in her life to again navigate the outside world, accomplishing such major things as buying her own groceries at the little Defensa Economica, a neighborhood store, or making her own way to her physical therapy appointments. Soon Laura would be joined by another woman who also made very good use of this respite environment.

Pat, an advocate at Casa Myrna, also worked weekends at the Salvation Army shelter, Harbor Light Center. One day she called me saying that there was a woman staying there that she thought would be appropriate for the overflow space. I was able to go over that day and meet Elizabeth.

We sat in a tiny office at Harbor Light Center. I could hear the worship service starting in another room, a small enough obligation for cold and hungry people in exchange for a good meal and a bed for the night. I heard the words of the preacher as he proclaimed something about faith, hope, and love.

Elizabeth smoked a lot (as did I at that time) and she also coughed a lot, suffering from a bad cold. She was not particularly friendly. She was not unfriendly, more like beaten down and exhausted. She was an older woman, probably in her early sixties, and appeared quite frail. I heard a little of her story and decided to accept her, especially given Pat's recommendation. Elizabeth gathered her scant belongings, and we rode to the shelter with little conversation. She looked stunned when she saw that she really would have her own room and bed and she immediately retired there.

After a couple of days and nights of being warm and

sleeping, Elizabeth recovered in body and spirit. She launched into care of the new shelter space, helping Laura and doing any other tasks that I might have. Laura enjoyed having the company and the two women got along well, sharing meals and stories and creating a cheerful, if temporary, home for themselves.

During those first days Elizabeth told me more and more of her story. She had been abused by her psychiatrist husband at their home in Philadelphia. She ran away and ended up in Boston because of a job opportunity. However, on the job she had a seizure and was deemed unable to do the work and lost the job. She applied for Supplemental Security Income (SSI) disability insurance and was approved, but her resources ran out before the checks came in and she lost her home. Alcohol had played a role in Elizabeth's life, but I did not know that at the time, and she was clearly now capable, intelligent, responsible, and sober.

Elizabeth also gave me an education about living on the street. For the last few weeks she had joined other people without homes, some of them mentally ill or addicted to drugs or alcohol, others just hard on their luck for a variety of reasons. She slept alongside others in large rooms at Rosie's Place, a shelter for homeless women, or Harbor Light or Shelter in Cambridge. Those were the good nights.

Since at that time there were many more people without homes in Boston than shelter beds, Elizabeth would periodically use up her limit of days at one of them and be on the street for the night. She huddled with other homeless women in warm spots near buildings. She learned ways to make it through winter nights, to sleep in the sheltered nooks and crannies of the Boston Public Library in Copley Square. She knew the locations of outdoor heat. She discovered how to hide in bus stations and how to pretend to be awaiting a late plane at the airport. Elizabeth learned the city hospital routine, when and for how long she could hang out in the waiting room without being noticed. She did this for several weeks during one period as she waited for a disability check to come.

Elizabeth was excited to be part of this effort to create a new shelter and while she was in the Franklin Square Ministry she basically functioned as the first volunteer staff person. I trusted her and she was enormously helpful. She and Laura shared resources, cooking, shopping, and eating together. And I will be forever grateful to Elizabeth for her help with Corrine, who joined the other two in creating a little community.

Corrine was referred by a good-hearted but unreliable source. I was told about a woman who had not been able to pay her rent and had been evicted. She had a nine-year-old son who was taken into custody by the Department of Social Services (DSS) because of their homelessness and she was quite distraught over this. The referring person begged me to take her, describing her as a sweet woman who had simply lost her home. Although I did not know the man referring her and had no connection to his agency, I accepted Corrine and learned a hard lesson.

Corrine was a large woman in her forties who seemed understandably upset at the loss of her home and her son. She was grateful for the space and in the beginning, she was friendly and cooperative. Laura and Elizabeth welcomed her and helped her to settle in. Our little shelter space was now full, with three women whose complex and interesting life stories had led at some point to them being without homes. For a brief time, they made a home for one another. I often stopped by the shelter to find the three engaged in conversation, laughing, sharing a meal. For a brief moment in time, it was a tiny beloved community. It foreshadowed the possibility of old and young, black and white, abled and physically challenged, helping one another and living in peace. It is what we hope for, a glimpse of a "kin-dom" of God not yet here, but envisioned. Sadly, it was not to last.

Corrine and I had several conversations and I accompanied her to a court hearing regarding custody of her son. My specific purpose was to let the judge understand that the child could come to the shelter with his mother while they looked for housing. Corrine had been there several days at that time and got along well with Elizabeth and Laura, who were both happy to welcome the child.

The court hearing took place in a private room. An older, friendly judge presided and listened with interest and compassion to the social workers, to Corrine, and then to me. The lawyer for the DSS claimed that Corrine was not capable of caring for her son and they sought permanent custody. The loss of this apartment, they said, was the last straw after numerous chances they had given her to provide a stable home for the child.

I was not aware of her history, I said, but I was willing to help her find a new home and to work with social workers to see that she had the support that she needed. I explained that she was in a safe shelter space that would welcome the child. The judge responded to me, quoting something in German, then translating into English. "When you lose hope, you lose everything," he said. While he did not agree to let the child join his mother at that time, he did continue a temporary custody order for the DSS rather than rule on a permanent one.

At Franklin Square Ministry things were looking up for both Laura and Elizabeth. Suzanne had found a place for

Laura, and Elizabeth's check had come with retroactive payments. She was able to find a nice little apartment in the Fenway. Both of them were preparing to move, while Corrine's behavior began to change. One day someone came to the door to give me our phone bill, which had been delivered to the wrong address. Corrine saw me with an envelope and asked me what it was. When I told her, she looked as if she didn't believe me, glared at me, went to her room, and slammed the door. After that she barely spoke to me.

Elizabeth told me that Corrine had become more and more secretive, and I could see that Laura was staying clear of her. Laura would never complain, especially if it caused another person to lose her shelter space, but she had enough street wisdom to avoid what might be a problem. Elizabeth and I conferred and agreed that Corrine was not well and that it was possibly not even safe for her or others that she stay. Since Laura and Elizabeth were leaving, we decided that we would close the rooms altogether and reconsider how, and if, to run things without resident staff. Corrine was not speaking to me or to Elizabeth and she left immediately upon hearing that we were closing. In cleaning her room, I found evidence of drug use and a hammer that had been missing.

Laura and Elizabeth had peaceful days in their new homes, but then had more difficulties. Laura's landlady decided that she was not comfortable with Laura's level of ability and asked her to leave. Rather than go through the search again or fight the eviction, Laura decided to move to New York to live with family. She had been estranged from them for years, in part over her relationship with the man who injured her, but now she and her family had reconciled. Laura wanted to be independent and would continue her slow but steady recovery, determined to be strong and free. Elizabeth continued to help at the shelter for several months, but she eventually took on other interests and we lost touch.

Corrine returned to the streets, spending many nights at Rosie's Place, where she exhibited increasingly disturbing behavior. Finally, one night she attacked my friend, Valerie Lanier, the director of Rosie's. She attacked Val with a mallet that she had hidden in her clothing and left her badly bruised. Valerie called the state Department of Mental Health and had Corrine committed for seventy-two hours, which was the only "care" that she would receive for her mental illness and addiction. During that time, they diagnosed her as "permanently psychotic and untreatable." They medicated her and returned her to the streets. A few months later an elderly woman in Roxbury took Corrine into her home. Sadly, one day Corrine attacked the woman who had offered her kindness, killing her with a hammer. I do not know what happened to her son.

I remembered a brief moment in the history of the shelter when three women gathered to form a little community, to listen to one another and to help one another. A young woman who was temporarily disabled but courageously trying to regain her health and her life; a middle-aged mother who had lost her child, initially hoping to have him back and to try again; and an older woman who put her tumultuous life experience into action to help the others. I was horrified to think what might have happened had Corrine's mental illness progressed more quickly, and was grieved to hear what ultimately did happen with Corrine and the kind woman who saw the deserving child of God in her.

In 1980, as I describe later, what had been the overflow space for Casa Myrna gained a few more rooms, an advisory committee, a full-time advocate, and about ten volunteer staff members, including an overnight person for every night. This was early in the domestic violence movement and people were eager to be a part of women helping other women in this way. And so we became Renewal House. It was a shelter for women in crisis and their children, a mission a little broader than for only victims of domestic violence, although that was our primary purpose.

One day soon after this, I was surprised by a call from Elizabeth, who asked if we could meet. We sat in the office where we had shared so many ideas and hopes and dreams, so many conversations with tears or laughter, where we had struggled with difficult and painful decisions and where Laura, Elizabeth, and Corrine had so briefly been a little community. There Elizabeth shared with me that she had lost her home, without being clear about how it had happened. Then she shared that she had, as she said, "the big C." Now Elizabeth was homeless with advanced lung cancer, and she asked to come back to the shelter.

The Renewal House staff welcomed her with warmth, and she moved in with the other women in crisis. She was not well enough to help out this time, but others were more than willing to help her. Elizabeth was lovingly cared for by both staff and guests. A Redemptorist priest from the Catholic residence nearby, respectful of the confidentiality of the shelter, came to give her Communion during her few weeks among us. One day Elizabeth and I traveled by ambulance to the hospital, where within a day or two she died. Elizabeth had experienced many changes in her life, many ups and certainly some downs. In her last years she was able to be of service to others, and in the end she was surrounded by people who cared for her with respect and affection. I participated in Elizabeth's funeral at the big Mission Hill Basilica, giving the eulogy in a Catholic mass led by the Redemptorist priest. The directors from the funeral home across the street, which did many services in this historically Irish Catholic neighborhood were confused about what to call me, seeing the clergy collar. After trying Father, then Mother, they finally settled on Reverend. In the true sense of the ministry at large, Elizabeth's estranged daughter was in touch with me after the funeral, and I later officiated at her wedding.

Prayerfully I see another baptism scene, and I remember words from Catholic priest and author Henri Nouwen: "We are the beloved. We are intimately loved long before our parents, teachers, spouses, children and friends loved or wounded us. That's the truth of our lives. That's the truth I want you to claim for yourself. That's the truth spoken by the voice that says, 'You are my Beloved.'"

Laura went down to the river, one might say she danced her way down to the river. She was a beautiful young woman filled with life and determined to live it with meaning. She practically dove into the water for the baptism. The cool water nourished her and she rejoiced with the feeling, but was surprised when she broke the surface and saw the brilliant sky. It was the dove that landed on her hand that surprised her most, and that voice of Light proclaiming, "This is my child." The voice said, "This is Laura, my beloved."

Elizabeth, too, went to the river as a young mother; her children played with the others while she allowed herself to be led by the prophet into the moving waters. She almost lost her balance and she laughed, confident that she was safe. And after the baptism it seemed somehow natural for the bird to appear and the voice to be heard. It filled and surrounded her with joy, and she felt embraced with the words, "This is my child, this is my beloved." Elizabeth was the beloved of the Holy.

Corrine, strong and clear and peaceful, also came to the waters. A self-assured woman with an abundance of life, with dreams of love and service, she too came for the holy baptism. She saw heavenly visions as she was submerged... light and angels and other realms...she was a seer after all. And yes, as she came up from the waters, yes...there was that voice, with the dove, loud and clear, "Corrine, Corrine, you are my beloved. Pay attention, world, and take care of this woman. She is the very beloved child of God."

There were many others that day, a little boy and an elderly woman from Roxbury, and a woman who could barely stand to put down her book. They came also to the waters, and they too were pronounced by the universe, by Being itself, to be the very beloved of God.

Dancing in the Firehouse

People came from miles around to hear Jesus. Some of them left their homes in haste to find him, hearing that he was in the area. They had heard that he could heal people by touching them and drive out demons with a word. In addition, what they heard about his teaching was strange but very appealing. That day it seemed like thousands of people joined those of us who were traveling with Jesus.

Jesus addressed the large crowd and spoke of the kingdom of God. He said it was breaking into the world even now! In fact, he said that it was among us already, even within us. He reminded us of the greatest two commandments. "Love God," he said, "with your heart, soul, mind, and strength. And love one another. This is how you will bring the kingdom to fullness. Love one another." And Jesus told us to forgive one another, to forgive over and over if need be. "Love even your enemies," he said. And he told us that as we did this we were already loved and forgiven. That seemed pretty impossible to some of us, but somehow when Jesus said it, we believed it.

As evening came Jesus told us that the speeches were over, it was time for us to eat and that after eating he needed to wander off for a bit of quiet time with his Abba God. One of his followers informed him that many of the people had failed to bring any food with them, and the nearest store or inn was miles away. "You give them something to eat," he said.

There were thousands of people, and we certainly didn't know how to give them something to eat when our own resources were so limited. "Feed the people," Jesus said.

"We want to, Jesus, but we don't know how." (Imagined from Matthew 14:16, Luke 6:27, Luke 17:21)

I was shocked to hear that Peggy was slipping out of the shelter at night and going to the local firehouse. Kate had been covering for her. But when Kate found out that Peggy was "dancing" at the firehouse she decided that she had to tell me.

"What do you mean she's 'dancing'?" I asked, having pictures in my mind of a DJ at the firehouse, and firefighters passing the time with a bit of popular dancing. "Are they having parties at the firehouse?"

"Uh, no, Peggy's dancing…strip dancing…stripping, even using the fire pole as a center for her routine. And now I think that she's involved with one of the firemen."

"Involved?"

"Sleeping with him. And he's married."

"Oh my God. You're telling me that teenaged Peggy is slipping out from the Franklin Square shelter space at night, stripping and dancing at a firehouse, sleeping with a married fireman! Anything else?"

"I think she might be pregnant."

Peggy and Kate were shelter guests of the early Franklin Square Ministry. Kate was a very together young white woman with a baby, who had been thrown out of her house by her alcoholic mother who objected to her interracial relationship. Danny, the African American father of her baby, was very much in the picture, but did not have a place for them to live. So, Kate was at the shelter while she and Danny saved money for an apartment. Kate's general common sense and compassion made her a good resident "staff member," and she had agreed to keep an eye on Peggy, but things had obviously gotten out of hand.

Peggy was an emancipated minor at the age of seventeen. The Department of Social Services had determined that the best course of action for her, given the unhappy and volatile relationship she had with her immigrant parents, was that she be considered independent. Various foster homes had not fared well, for Peggy ran away from them all. At seventeen she could legally be on her own, but she had no income and no place to live. One of my trusted social workers asked if she could come stay at FSM while they worked on finding her a job and a home.

Every evening I would take my dog Chouchou out for a walk and she would run happily to the shelter door as we stopped by to make sure everything was okay. Apparently, Peggy would wait for my evening check on the shelter, and after Chouchou and I had gone she would leave for her night-time activity. Kate had been distressed that Peggy was slipping out, but she didn't want Peggy to be kicked out of the shelter and she had initially believed that Peggy was not doing anything harmful. She had gained Peggy's trust and now Peggy was confiding in her; Kate felt that she was Peggy's only friend. When she first learned of the firehouse activity, she tried to convince Peggy of the foolishness and danger of her actions, but to no avail.

Finally, she told Peggy that she would have to tell me. And then Peggy revealed that she was pregnant.

I knew that an immediate response was called for, but I had no idea what to do. Of course, I told Peggy that her trips to the firehouse had to stop. I shared my reactions with her, including my outrage at the firefighters who had allowed this young girl to behave in this way. I had visions of going to the firehouse myself to confront these men. Or should I call the fire department and report them? Or the police? Peggy begged me not to do any of this, sounding truly desperate, and I was most concerned for her well-being. I decided that I would take up the issue with my co-ministers at the staff meeting the next day and get advice.

Before I could do anything, however, I was awakened in the night by Kate calling to say that Peggy was bleeding and seemed to be having a miscarriage. I rushed her to the hospital where it became certain that she would lose the child. That night in the hospital, Peggy, the emancipated "woman," was so clearly a very young girl. She was a child losing her child, whom she had hoped would be somebody to love her—a teenager, abandoned and alone. Peggy was devastated by the pain and the loss. Because my own child was staying overnight with a friend, I was able to spend most of the night with her, and when it was all over and she was asleep, I went home for a little sleep myself.

The next day I visited Peggy in the hospital and while I was there her "lover" and another firefighter came to visit her. It was an awkward experience for all. The man who had gotten Peggy pregnant was kind and compassionate toward her and was obviously deeply ashamed in front of me. I learned that prior to this time he had made clear to Peggy that it was a mistake to be involved with her; that he cared about her; that he was very sorry; and that he could not see her again. He had told her that she must not come to the firehouse. He did not know of the pregnancy until she called that morning, when he rushed over to see her, devastated.

Both firefighters assured me that there would be no more parties. Peggy begged me not to pursue the matter further and made clear that she would deny any accusations. Ultimately, after consulting with others including a lawyer and Peggy's social worker, I decided not to report this situation. I considered Peggy's fragile state, believing that, at least, the two firefighters were frightened and sorry that they had allowed and participated in these activities. Such decisions are difficult and painful to make and require weighing the wellbeing of an individual vs. the social/moral issue. The firefighters might well have thought that Peggy was older than she was—from what they said I believe that they did—but she was a teenager, and even if she were older, they were exploiting her mental instability. Nevertheless, I judged that she was not in a mental state to go through the reporting. I hoped that the fear of a report and the shame they exhibited would prevent the firefighters from engaging in such activities in the future.

Peggy returned to the shelter filled with an unbearable sense of emptiness and loss. Kate, the social worker, and I did our best to comfort and encourage her, but soon Peggy reacted by trying to end the pain forever.

I received a frantic call from Kate. "What should I do? Peggy has taken a bottle of prescription Benadryl and some other pills that she had in her room. She's conscious but stumbling around in a daze." I repeated what she said, trying to get a clear picture, but before I could recommend action my twelve-year-old daughter Rachel, overhearing the conversation and seeing me pause, said, "Call an ambulance, Mom. Call an ambulance!" Quickly I instructed Kate, "Call an ambulance immediately and I'll be right over."

The ambulance came promptly from one of the nearby hospitals, and as the very impressive EMTs ran in, Peggy went into a seizure. The first responders took charge, laying her on the floor, giving her an IV, and hooking her up to monitors which were in communication with the hospital. While they were monitoring her the shelter phone rang and, since it was on the other side of Peggy's prone body, one of the EMTs picked it up and handed it to me. "Is Peggy there?" a male voice said. I simply said no, but standing there with the phone stretched across her body and various monitors beeping, I wanted to respond, "I don't know, let me check the heart monitor."

The EMTs were directed to nearby Children's Hospital, which I thought was appropriate for this teenager. Peggy was treated and kept overnight. She was to be released the next day, but the hospital would not release her to an unsupervised situation. Her family wanted nothing to do with her and she could not return to the shelter with only Kate and her baby present.

I was due to host a group of Unitarian Universalist seminarians at a camp outside of the city, owned and run by the Ben Frat. In its heyday, Camp Parker was a summer camp, but suburban sprawl had made it less appealing, and the programs had changed. Nevertheless, it was a good place for small gatherings such as this, with cabins and a meeting room on a small lake. The former director's cabin was nice and roomy, and Rachel and I had stayed there in the past. Peggy's doctor felt that the crisis had passed, but that Peggy could not be alone, so Rachel stayed overnight with a friend while Peggy accompanied me for the night at Camp Parker. Peggy slept while I gave a presentation to the seminarians on urban ministry and spoke specifically about a beautiful young woman who needed to be loved, changing her name and enough of her circumstances to protect her privacy.

Peggy was very subdued over the weekend, and when we returned to Boston, she began a regular counseling relationship with Ann Fawcett, the new shelter intern counselor. A social worker found Peggy a room in a nice house in a quiet community where, sadly, she attempted suicide again. On that occasion Peggy called Kate, who called the ambulance again, and she was hospitalized and released. However, the landlady was alarmed and asked Peggy to leave. She ended up living in a rougher community north of Boston, where she pursued her "career" as a dancer.

Peggy stopped keeping in touch with any of us—the social

worker, Ann, me, even Kate. But one day a year or two later she called me and asked for help. She'd had a dispute with her employer and needed to get her paycheck but was afraid to go there by herself. My fiancé, Graylan, had moved to Boston by that time and we went together to the dirty, depressing, little club. While the manager went to the back office for the check, we watched a young girl try to be hot and sexy, barely clad, while twirling around a pole or writhing on the floor. Fat, sleazy men sat around her and alternated between making disgusting noises and ignoring the young woman while they drank their whiskey and talked. When these white men saw Graylan, who is black, we could feel the tension rising and became very uncomfortable. Fortunately, the man came with Peggy's check at just the right time. There was no art or beauty in that place. There was no joy. There was no respect for any of the precious human life gathered there.

Peggy and I visited briefly, and she assured me that she was doing well. She said that she had decided to give up her "career" as a dancer and to do something that didn't involve leering, intoxicated men. She had been back in touch with the social worker who had helped her before, and they were looking into job-training programs. I wished her good luck.

I loved Peggy for a time, and I loved Kate, who had her own whole story (I later officiated at her wedding to her baby's father!). I believe that they are part of my being. I am different because I loved them; they informed me and transformed me. Through their eyes I saw different worlds than those that I had experienced before, and I gained an expanded and deeper understanding of the challenges and pain facing many in our society. I was privileged to know these two beautiful, brave, creative young women. Through the years of ministry at large I loved many people, sometimes very briefly as they entered and left my life. Sometimes we had relationships for years. My heart was broken at times, and

I was always nourished by their beauty and uniqueness.

Peggy was a vivacious, gutsy, bold, original young woman. She needed to be fed and cared for and some of us tried: the counselors, the social workers, the friends, even boyfriends. We wanted to feed Peggy and to care for her. And all we knew how to do was to try our best, to remain faithful and available, and then be there again for the next person who comes to the shelter.

We don't know how to feed them, Jesus. We see that the people have left their homes and that they have no food. We care about that… We care about the runaway child pretending to be an adult, seeking attention and love in destructive ways. We care. but how do we feed her? How do we nourish her? We care about the young woman and baby with no home and we care about her alcoholic mother and the baby's father. We are willing to feed the people. We want to feed them. Please show us how, Jesus, please show us how.

"Love one another," he said. "Love one another. Keep trying! Do it again. Love again, love some more. The food will be there if you have love for one another." (Imagined from Matthew 14:16, Luke 6:27, Luke 17:21)

Golgotha: A Good Friday Story

On that Friday three people died violently, horribly, crucified. The women sat at the foot of the cross where Jesus had sighed his last sigh and they wailed. His male disciples were a distance away, terrified and grieved. They too cried and saw an empty, devastating future.

Two other men died as well. Perhaps there were women at the base of their crosses, or in the distance, or home grieving and angry and lost. We are not told. The story is that they were robbers, or perhaps they were insurrectionists. As one of them said, they were not innocent men. Jesus was innocent of any crime; they were not. They were men with complicated lives, had made bad choices perhaps, or their intentions had gone awry. (Imagined from Mark 15:25–27)

We sat in a dingy district courtroom waiting for the probable cause hearing. The room was filled with unhappy, frightened, or bored-looking people. Some were there for cases, victims, or defendants. Some were prosecutors and defense attorneys with too many cases; clerks with administrative roles; security guards looking around at the same old thing—people and their many problems, people out of control. Greed, violence, stupidity. Same old thing.

It was my first time in court as a companion and advocate. Diane sat beside me, bruises on her face and a big gap where a front tooth belonged. They were charging her husband with assault and battery with a dangerous weapon, a shod foot. That was a felony and if probable cause was found, the charges would go to the superior court. We watched as case after case was called: robberies, assaults, breaking and entering. And then it was Diane's turn. "O'Neill," the clerk called out.

Frank O'Neill stood and stepped forward along with the police detective to whom Diane had gone with her report of the beating, and the district attorney who hurriedly looked at the charges. Diane had not seen Frank in the courthouse before now and she began to tell me again, loudly and in colorful language, what he had done to her and just what she thought of him. Frank turned around and looked at her as the judge ordered her to be quiet. He was indeed a big man, with a scar running across his face from an old bar fight. He was acting humbly, but his very presence suggested that he was not someone to mess with.

The charges were read, the detective testified, and then it was Frank's turn to respond. No, he said, this was not true, he had never hit his wife. They had been drinking and she had fallen. His story was interrupted by Diane's shouts: "Liar, son of a bitch, you lie! You hit me and kicked me over and over! Look at my tooth, he knocked out my front tooth!"

"Quiet in the court," the judge said as he used his gavel to bring order. "If you cannot restrain yourself you will have to leave the courtroom! This is a final warning." The bored people in the room began to perk up and smile and watch: "Oh, good, a little action in this endless routine of sad, repetitive stories." Diane's bruises added some color to the picture.

The judge determined that the case should go to a grand jury at the superior court to determine the charges. And on to the next case, and the next, and the next.

I had tried to help Diane remain calm, but she was barely in control as her rage and pain spilled out at the sight of Frank. We gave the detective a ride back to his station and then I took Diane back to the shelter where she was staying, Casa Myrna, where I had begun to volunteer prior to opening the new shelter; I had been asked to be the advocate for this wounded, broken, angry, beaten woman.

Diane did indeed have a drinking problem, as I later

understood, but she regained her self-control and poise over the days of being safe and sober. I took her to my dentist for a new front tooth and spent time with her, getting to know her and encouraging her. She was determined to see the charges against Frank go forward. The violence had escalated, and she was afraid that unless he was in prison, he would ultimately kill her. She had tried to leave him more than once; he always found her and convinced her to come back to him. But as much as she hated him, Diane said she also loved him. His violence was not the whole story. He was a complicated and lovable person most of the time, she said, but then suddenly, especially when he was drunk, he would turn on her violently. Later, she would be vulnerable to his pleas for forgiveness and his promises of change.

Diane told me only a little about her background. She had grown up in a wealthy suburb in the western part of the state. She was estranged from her parents and spoke disdainfully about the values of this affluent community. She had run away from home at least once as a teen. From all that she told me I suspected that she had been sexually abused.

Diane told me more about Frank's history. He had grown up in a working-class neighborhood of Boston and had been brutally beaten by his father. He had a history of violence. Diane told me that he had killed a man in a fight, throwing him down a flight of stairs. He had been in prison on another charge and had ended up in Bridgewater State Hospital, the prison for offenders with mental health problems. Frank had been judged to be violent and dangerous when under the influence of alcohol. Diane persisted in getting her life and health back while preparing to testify to the grand jury.

One day Diane did not return to Casa Myrna. Eventually she called and said that on her way to a doctor's appointment she had run into Frank. She told me that he had forced her to join him, but not to worry. With the grand jury scheduled he would be afraid to do her any harm. She had told Frank that she would go into the hearing and tell them that he had not hurt her. She assured me that he needed her to be willing to do that, so she was safe. Then, she said, she actually would go into the grand jury and tell them exactly what he had done. Frank would be arrested, tried, and convicted and she would be free.

Diane wanted to come by Casa Myrna and get her things, but the staff did not trust her to come without Frank, and the confidentiality of shelters was critical in protecting everyone. I said that I would take her things and arrange to meet her. It was my fervent hope that in doing so I would be able to help her escape again. I thought that she might agree to go to the Franklin Square Ministry space that we were using as overflow for Casa Myrna. Its location would still be confidential. "Dangerous while under the influence of alcohol," I remembered; Frank pushing someone down the stairs and killing him; Diane's bruised and battered face when I first met her.

I met Diane in a safe place, and we went to my apartment for her belongings. Sadly, it was clear that Diane was quite intoxicated and not at all interested in my idea of going to the overflow shelter space. She agreed to sit and talk with me, but she said that Frank would always find her, she could not hide forever, she had to live her life. She tried to convince me that she was in control of the whole situation, that Frank would not hurt her as long as the grand jury hearing hung over his head. "He is terrified of prison," she said, "and he believes that I will go into the grand jury and tell them that he has never hurt me. He won't touch me until then."

I suggested to Diane that if shelter in Boston would not work, she could consider going home to her family. She would be safe there; Frank would not dare follow her. Police in wealthy communities do not like violent strangers threatening people in their towns.

Diane seemed to think this was a possibility and I convinced her to call her parents. I asked her if she wanted me to do it, using the reverend title and telling them that their daughter really was in need of their help, but she said no, she would do it. Diane called home and her mother answered. She said that she was in danger, was taking Frank to court, and she asked if she could come home. When her mother did not immediately agree Diane became belligerent and swore at her mother, sounding very intoxicated. I don't know who hung up first. In spite of my pleas Diane took her things and went back to Frank.

There was no word from her for weeks as the grand jury date approached. Then one day I received a call from a detective. It was a normal morning. I had just seen Rachel off to the school bus and had walked the dog. The phone rang and it was Detective Finnell. "Hello Reverend," he said. "I have some news for you regarding Diane O'Neill. I'm sorry to tell you, it's not good news." He told me that Diane had been found drowned. Her body had floated to the surface of a local city pond. People out rowing on Jamaica Pond on a spring day had been horrified when the oar hit what turned out to be a human body, one that had once been a lovely, vibrant, complicated, mixed-up human being—Diane.

I was stunned and shocked. It was incomprehensible to me. Diane had been sitting in my kitchen. We had talked about Frank being dangerous, about his having killed someone. People actually do kill each other, I know that. It is a fact. There are stories in the paper, stories that people tell each other, every day. Every day. But no, goddamn it, no. Not this! This was Diane. She was sitting here in my kitchen not long before, with me begging her to stay. This was real. But no, what had been Diane—spirited, angry, determined, and addicted Diane—was now a lifeless body that had floated up to the surface of Boston's lovely Jamaica Pond.

The story of what happened unfolded. There had been a group of men and women hanging out at Jamaica Pond, a beautiful city pond, living on the banks. They were addicts and alcoholics, Frank, Diane, and another woman, who was apparently Frank's girlfriend, among them. The girlfriend entered a drug detox center not long after the body was found, and while she was detoxing, she said that she had seen Frank kill Diane. "He held her under until the bubbles stopped," she said. The counselor called the police, but by that time the woman was sober again and she denied it. The specific description of the drowning, however, "the bubbles stopping," convinced Detective Finnell of the truthfulness of the story, and he kept the investigation open. He also continued to pursue the grand jury on the original assault and battery complaint. He had pictures of Diane's badly bruised face and her testimony. At least he could pursue that. At least the threat of that could continue to hang over Frank's head. At least that.

The grand jury did indict Frank on a felony assault charge, but since there was no witness, eventually the charges were dropped.

I saw Frank and the girlfriend, who had returned to Frank and was no longer clean and sober, twice after that. I'm not sure where they were living or if they had returned to the banks of Jamaica Pond. Once I saw them in a restaurant, a little lunch place in my neighborhood. They were sitting at a table eating, and I watched as Frank dribbled his food down his face. "Mainliners," the waitress said with disgust. Heroin addicts. They were both so high they could barely eat. On another day I saw them both stumbling down the street, again totally "wasted." And I thought, "Yes, they are wasted. What a sad thing. Wasted human beings."

Diane was the first abused woman for whom I had advocated in my ministry at large. I cared about her. I had seen her beaten and bruised, out of control in the courtroom, recovering her health and sobriety. I had seen her enraged and drunk and determined. I had seen her light and laughing and hopeful. She was someone who had been wounded in life and she responded from her pain. Like all of us she was a wounded and conflicted human being, and she was worthy of life, a chance to be the bright charming person that she could be.

Now I was the one who was angry. Of course, I wanted Frank to be held accountable. You can't just kill people with no consequence. And this poor woman who was with him now, lost and helpless in her addiction and certainly terrified of Frank, she deserved a chance too. And how were we to protect others from this violent, out-of-control man? Why had he been free to beat and drown his wife in the first place? How could we protect women and other vulnerable people so they did not have to leave their homes and hide in confidential shelters? What was wrong with our society? With us?! I believe in the inherent worth and dignity of every person. I believe in the essential goodness of human beings, but sometimes amidst the violence it is very hard to see. Quakers talk about seeing "that of God" in every person, but as one Friend said, "I love that of God in that person, and very little else."

I was angry, but I found it hard to direct my anger toward Frank. He was just too wounded and destroyed. He was a beaten child who grew up to beat others. I knew that the little boy that Frank had been deserved a chance too. I was angry at the world, at the criminal justice system, angry at my own helplessness, and angry at God. I had felt a clear call to this ministry in community, to help people toward wholeness and freedom. Now I felt like a participant in the crucifixion! Where was God for Diane? For Frank? For the other addicted woman?

In twelve-step programs, such as Alcoholics Anonymous, they talk of a Higher Power that can help us to do what we cannot do by ourselves. But they say that when that Higher Power feels unavailable as God, then look to the group, the community, as the Higher Power. I had the grace to be working with committed and wonderful people. I was part of a team ministry at the Ben Frat. My co-minister at large, Scotty McLennan, especially, took time to listen to my anger and despair, to hear and share in my loss. Staff meetings with Scotty, Thom Payne, and Bud Murdock became times when we would share each other's challenges, losses, and joys. From the earliest days of the ministry at large it was clear how much we need and depend on one another in this work; how nothing is ever accomplished alone.

While I was angry at God, I had beloved colleagues and friends. Eventually I began to understand this as the meaning of incarnation. Theologically, incarnation refers to God's choice to be present in Jesus in a completely human way, to emphasize God's solidarity with humankind and God's presence in the body of humankind. God was there all the time in my friends, as well as in my own heart. God was not an absent being or impersonal force, but an intensely present, continuously creating force of love existing dynamically in all things, including us. The love that is God is personal and weeps in us and with us for the destruction and violence of our lives; shares in the crucifixions and brokenness; and encourages us to co-create a world where we can truly learn to love one another. And to sustain us in this difficult work of building a nonviolent world of justice and peace, God gives us one another.

I led an informal memorial service for Diane at Casa Myrna. Most of the other guests who had been present when Diane lived there had now moved on, hopefully to new homes, free from violence. Several of the new guests attended the memorial along with the staff. We remembered Diane's transformation from a beaten person to a hopeful, bright woman who had blossomed during her weeks in the shelter. We acknowledged the tragic loss. And the other women resolved that they would continue, committed in their own journeys to live productive lives free from violence. A year after Diane's death we opened Renewal House, where hundreds of other women and children have now found safety and a chance at new life.

Jesus was crucified that Friday along with the others. Crucifixion was a particularly cruel form of execution devised by the Roman Empire, It can serve as an appropriate symbol for the many cruelties of our world today. We can imagine that there was Diane on the cross to one side of Jesus, and Frank to the other side. There were others too on other crosses, women and men who were addicted to drugs and alcohol, and people who were poor and hungry. There were some who were mentally ill, some homeless; young people with no alternative to urban gangs; old people with no place to live. There were those who were simply in the wrong place at the wrong time, or the wrong gender or the wrong race, and a tragic number of children who had been beaten and abandoned. All these and more – the crosses extended into the distance as far as the eye could see – beloved children of God, like Jesus, being crucified by our failure to love one another. But God gives us another chance. We discover that the story of Jesus is not about death, but about life and resurrection. We have another chance. That's the point of the Christian story. We still have another chance to love one another.

Seek the Reign of God First, Part One

In that important speech that Jesus gave on the mountain (or was it on the plain?), he said, "Stop worrying then over questions such as, 'What are we to eat,' or 'What are we to drink,' or 'What are we to wear?' Those without faith are always running around after those things. God knows everything you need. Seek first God's reign, and God's justice, and all these things will be given to you besides. Enough of worrying about tomorrow. Let tomorrow take care of itself. Today has troubles enough of its own." (Imagined from Matthew 6:31-33, The Inclusive Bible)

During the first year of my ministry at large, the activities in the space that Franklin Square House had provided for women in crisis had operated under the name of the Franklin Square Ministry (FSM). Through the year of networking in the community and with other organizations and churches, a good number of women had become involved in this movement of women helping women who were experiencing domestic violence. By the fall of 1979 FSM had a number of active volunteers who functioned together as an advisory committee. There were representatives of several community advocacy agencies as well as women who had experienced domestic violence or other crises. Therefore, when the Franklin Square House offered us a newly available and larger space, we jumped at the chance to open a full-time shelter for women in crisis, primarily those escaping domestic violence.

We had minimal funding and resources, but great people power! Ann Fawcett had joined me for the academic year as an intern. I met Ann when giving an informal talk to UU seminarians at Harvard Divinity School and she had been excited about the idea of working with women who were victims of violence. When she joined me she had changed her focus to counseling and was interested in pursuing this work with women in crisis. Ann became critically involved with

Peggy and Kate and others. Her experience and wisdom were part of the basic foundation of the new, emerging shelter.

We had a modest grant from a Unitarian Universalist family and a pool of volunteers, including commitments of overnight stays from a number of women from the Boston Theological Institute, a network of seminaries. Women were grateful for the opportunity to help other women who were experiencing violence. Gracia Woodword volunteered to do fundraising; Sally, a woman from an affluent community, who had once herself been abused, offered her time and experience to do whatever we needed; Amarette Calloway offered to do childcare; and a neighborhood friend found us furniture from a renovated nursing home.

The advisory group gathered in excitement to lay out plans for the opening and to determine what else we would need. We had newsprint up on the office wall as we brainstormed names.

What were we, after all? We were safe space where women could rest, use resources, and reclaim their lives. "Okay…Reclamation House, no, Restoration House. Okay, I know, Revival, Revival House…to come alive again." We were excited about that name, but on second thought perhaps "revival" had other implications. As we brainstormed there was a lot of laughter, as there so often is when people gather together to do something they care so much about.

And then someone said "Renewal House" and there was enthusiastic agreement. Renewal House it was!

We assessed our needs and there was still a major one. We needed a full-time counselor/advocate to staff the shelter on weekdays and to oversee the advocacy. And although we were beginning formal fundraising and were completely optimistic, we had only $3000.

"Do not worry," Jesus said in his Sermon on the Mount, "...seek first God's reign and God's justice and all these things will be given to you as well." (Matthew 6:33) Seek the realm of God first. Seek peace and justice, create communities of love, heal the broken, feed the hungry, take in the homeless poor. Seek God's right way first and all that you need will follow.

I spoke to my friend Val Lanier, director of Rosie's Place, a shelter for homeless women, who had helped us already in many ways. And it happened that a friend of Val's, a nun, had just arrived in Boston and was looking for something to do. She would be partially supported by her community, but needed both ministry and a small income while she was in transition. Val's friend had been working with young nuns in Puerto Rico and planned on going to a mission in Latin America when she suffered a back injury and was unable to take the assignment. Now healed, she was seeking a new mission. And so Rita Brereton, SSND entered my life.

I fervently hoped that this nun, Rita, would work out, but of course there were many unknowns. The Roman Catholic women whom I had met in urban ministry were certainly socially progressive, if not radical, and were strong supporters of women. But she was a nun after all, and that was quite a different path than Unitarian Universalist ministry. I understood that the Roman Catholic church had very strong positions on marriage: it was considered a sacrament in the church. How would that be understood in a domestic violence situation? Would Rita be comfortable with women who sought to divorce their husbands?

Rita and I met in the living room of what was soon to be Renewal House. A lovely, outgoing woman in her thirties, Rita wondered what it would be like to work in a Unitarian Universalist setting. The idea of helping women flee violence appealed to her, as did working with them to create a new life free of violence. That would be a worthwhile ministry. But she didn't know much about Unitarians and what she had heard was confusing. They were a church, but they weren't Christians, she had been told. Okay, but what were they? So Rita and I each approached our first meeting cautiously. What would this nun be like? What did the Unitarian minister actually believe? However, any doubts about the other fell away quickly as we engaged in a spirited discussion and felt an immediate connection with one another.

Rita and I talked about the job description, and I was clear about the tiny stipend. Rita stressed that she could accept that for a few months, but that eventually she would have to seek a regular income. I assured her that we had begun fundraising. Rita told me about her background working with young nuns in Puerto Rico. She liked working with women and was interested in knowing more about domestic violence. As I told her some of my experiences over the past year, and the stories that I had heard from many women, she became righteously angry on their behalf. This righteous anger on behalf of others was something that I would see often. Justice and compassion had a way of merging powerfully in Rita.

As we explored the possibility of working together, I wanted to be sure of Rita's strong advocacy for women's rights and freedom; she wanted to be clear that she would not be asked to do things in opposition to her faith, specifically not to directly aid in abortion. We agreed that if such an issue came up, she would stand aside for someone else to handle it. She would not impose her beliefs, but she would expect to have them respected. As far as advocating for women's rights, Rita knew from her own church community what it was like to have less-than-full opportunity. She was a fierce advocate for women.

Our conversation during that first meeting went from

discussion of the specific job and women's issues to religion. I had begun to identify as a Universalist Christian and so I tried my best to describe that within a description of Unitarian Universalism. Rita was intrigued, as was I as I listened to her describe her own deeply held Christian faith. She felt perfectly free to criticize her church, as I felt free to criticize mine in areas with which I disagreed.

Rita lived with three other nuns in an apartment in Boston's Dorchester neighborhood. All of the sisters were engaged in challenging ministries, and they shared regular worship and prayer time with one another. I found myself very attracted to such a communal religious life, but I was not Catholic, and I believed in my own call to ordination as a Unitarian Universalist, so a religious community of that kind was not available. But I was intrigued.

I clarified with her, "So you are all working in the world, but you come home to eat together while sharing what you are doing in the context of faith, and regularly worship together?" It sounded wonderful to me. On the other hand, Rita felt powerfully called to ministry, aware that she would be a good priest, and she was questioning her commitment to her community, while remaining loyal to her Catholic heritage. We commiserated over the strange and opposite places in which we found ourselves longing. Something was missing in my life that I saw in the nun's life. Something was present in the Protestant minister's life that was missing in hers.

Rita and I met for that initial conversation early in 1980 and Renewal House formally opened on Valentine's Day of that year. In June, I met the man who would become my husband, and Rita stayed in Boston and in her vocation. We both followed the paths that had initially called us to ministry. After the first few months at Renewal House Rita felt called to ministry in a Catholic parish and became the pastoral associate at Holy Family Parish in Dorchester, a bilingual urban faith community in the neighborhood where my husband and I eventually settled. She did leave her religious community but remained a pastoral associate and loyal to the Roman Catholic church. Renewal House did well in its fundraising and was able to hire a full-time counselor/advocate—Amarette moved from her role as a childcare volunteer to advocate and was supplemented by student interns and dedicated volunteers, many of them representing different faiths.

One of the joys of working in urban ministry is the possibility, in fact the necessity, of interfaith work. We are brought together in our desire to create a just and peaceful community, and this enables us to be continually enriched by one another, and to be effective in the world. The Roman Catholic nun and the Unitarian Universalist clergywoman shared in a continuing and foundational search for God in our lives, sought ways to honor that God through service and worship, shared in the outrage over the violence and injustices of our community, and sought concrete ways to better love our neighbor.

After several years of ministry Rita developed a very aggressive breast cancer during the same time that I was leaving my ministry position. I was living alone at that time, and worship and dinners at the Holy Family rectory along with Rita's prayerful support offered me a sense of home and comfort. And weekly, Rita and I traveled the route from Dorchester, in inner city Boston, across the river to Cambridge for Reiki and healing prayer sessions for Rita with my friend Thomas Mikelson, minister at First Parish in Cambridge and Reiki master. (Reiki is a Japanese form of healing through the laying on of hands and the giving of "life force" energy.) I did not know when I first interviewed Rita that we were entering a sacred and eternal friendship which would take us through many journeys until her death in 2003. Grace brought us together in our mutual need, and the women and children of Renewal House received loving support and safe space because of it.

> *Therefore, do not worry saying, "What shall we eat?" or "What shall we wear?" Your heavenly father knows that you need those things. Seek first the kingdom of God and God's righteousness and all these things will be given you as well.*

Beating Swords into Plowshares

"They shall beat their swords into plowshares, and their spears into pruning hooks, nation shall not lift up sword against nation, neither shall they learn war anymore; but they shall sit under their own vines and under their own fig trees, and no one shall make them afraid; for the mouth of the Lord of hosts has spoken." (Micah 4:3b–4)

Two or three days before the opening date of Renewal House, in February of 1980, we received a call from an Episcopal priest in a nearby suburban community. His parishioner, Ronnie, was experiencing violence and he was very worried about her. She was a Vietnamese woman who had married a solider during the Vietnam War. A small woman, her large husband had recently dislocated her shoulder. While things were quiet in the household at present, the priest feared for her safety and the safety of their three-year-old son. Rita and I agreed that she could come to Renewal House as soon as possible; the priest would help her to escape. For several days we did not hear from them, but we held a room, hoping they would call. Finally, the priest had been able to reach Ronnie and to assist her in leaving home with her son, Daniel, and to bring them to Renewal House. Ronnie had managed to bring a suitcase of clothes and things for Danny and to leave while her husband, Matthew, was at work. She was frightened of what Matthew would do when he found that she had left. We assured her that she was safe, and he could not know where she was. She retired to her room and kept to herself.

The next day, the first order of business was to go to court for a restraining order and temporary custody of Daniel. According to the domestic violence law, an emergency restraining order had to be granted and a hearing held five days later, which could extend the order for a year, or dismiss it. We were told, however, that the judge of that district court was unavailable to grant the temporary order, and a hearing in which Matthew would be included was scheduled for that Friday.

On Friday it was obvious that the judge was sympathetic to Matthew and did not want to grant the order to protect Ronnie. Because I knew the law and perhaps because Ronnie's arm was in a sling, the judge did grant a restraining order for three months, and a custody order for the same period. He scheduled a custody hearing for the end of that time and ordered Ronnie to allow Matthew to see Daniel weekly for unsupervised visits. I explained that the shelter was in a confidential location for the women's safety. The judge said that that was not his concern and to work out meeting places with Matthew. We learned then from Ronnie that her father-in-law, Matthew's father, was a well-respected police captain in that community and a friend of the judge's. That explained his reluctance to be helpful to Ronnie.

The first visit was a nightmare, as were several subsequent visits. We arranged to meet Matthew in front of a nearby police station. Daniel went off with his father for the day and Ronnie and I returned at the agreed upon time to pick him up, but they were not there. After frantic calls to his parents and others Matthew came more than an hour late. He objected to meeting at the police station and we agreed to meet at a church not far from the shelter so that volunteers without cars could accompany Ronnie at appointed times. It was also a very public place where we assumed that Matthew would not make trouble.

During one pickup time an older volunteer, who was the librarian at a nearby seminary, accompanied Ronnie. After picking up Daniel, they walked a roundabout way back to the shelter, Ronnie carrying a sleeping Daniel. However, after a block or so the volunteer saw that Matthew was following them. He shouted to them angrily saying that they should not be walking around this neighborhood, that it was not safe, and he offered them money for a cab. The volunteer, who had no money with her, took the money and they flagged a cab, which they directed to drive around for a while, realizing that Matthew had continued to follow them. They got out of the cab in a busy area, went into a restaurant and then out the back door and down an alley. They took back streets home, managing to lose Matthew. Daniel slept through the entire trip. The volunteer wrote in our log that she was not in the habit of leading young women down dark alleys, that she didn't normally venture down them herself, but it seemed the best course of action under the circumstances!

The problem with meeting Matthew in the vicinity of Renewal House was that eventually three-year-old Daniel pointed out his new home to his father. Matthew began to hang around outside, hoping to intersect with Ronnie, and harassing Rita as she came to work. Rita had been appointed as the person to arrange visits and deal with Matthew on the telephone, and he began calling her at her home, cursing and shouting at her. Rita scheduled a new court hearing and went to see the judge. While she hardly fit the stereotype of a shy and retiring nun, Rita was perfectly happy to use the symbolic power of her vocation in certain circumstances, especially when defending someone else.

So Sister Rita, SSN told the Irish Catholic judge that she was a nun, that Matthew was harassing her when she came to work, and that he was calling her "convent" (officially the home of even a few nuns living together) and cursing at the sisters, who were frightened and upset. For the first time the judge took notice and ordered Matthew to stop calling and to stay away from the shelter, threatening to cut off visitation if he did not behave. Sadly, the judge did allow the visits to continue.

In the meantime, Ronnie took the necessary steps to continue with her life. Initially we encouraged her to sign up for welfare and food stamps. She was very reluctant to do this and wanted to work, but it was a matter of "first things first." The new laws on domestic violence were designed to make it easy for women to sign up for aid since many of them stayed in violent situations because they had no financial alternative. (The welfare "reform" laws have since changed this.) It was a temporary measure for Ronnie and with our help she was able to pursue job training as a home healthcare worker. Through our Unitarian Universalist member churches, we found a lawyer who would take her case pro bono and Ronnie started divorce proceedings.

Daniel's visits with Matthew continued and Matthew's parents became more involved, which made everyone a bit more comfortable with the situation—although on one occasion Matthew kept Daniel several days longer than arranged while staying with his parents. Ronnie was alarmed but trusted her in-laws, and Matthew communicated daily in a peaceful manner.

On another occasion, however, Matthew did not bring Daniel home and there were no phone calls. Rita called Matthew's parents and discovered that they had not seen or heard from him. They were alarmed. Rita went to the suburban court once more and reported Matthew's disappearance with Daniel. The judge (a bit late!), finally accepted the idea that Matthew was unstable and that this was a dangerous situation for the child. He put out a warrant for Matthew's arrest and ordered Daniel's return and an end to the visitations! But nobody heard from Matthew.

Weeks went by and there was no call or word from Matthew. Ronnie was devastated, and the whole shelter with her, but she courageously took the next steps for life together with her son. She found a job and an apartment in a nearby community and began to prepare for her move, to find appropriate furnishings for Daniel's new room. She was baptized and active in the Episcopal church, which continued to support her. She "kept the faith." The lives of the other women and children in the shelter continued with the daily dramas, court appearances, anxieties, talking and listening, and efforts to find housing. Everyone embraced Ronnie and prayed for Daniel's well-being.

In July I led a workshop on faith development at Star Island, a UUA and UCC conference center off the coast of New Hampshire. I treasured the journeys of the people who attended, but my heart remained heavy, thinking of Ronnie and Daniel. One morning as I arrived bleary-eyed for morning coffee someone told me that there was a phone message for me on the message board. There was only a radio phone on the island at that time and calls were limited to emergencies. I retrieved the message, which said simply "Daniel has been found safe. Rita." I shouted with joy and told all around me that a child who was lost had been found! I went to the office where they let me call Rita on the radio phone and she recounted the story of retrieving Daniel. Matthew had called Renewal House in the middle of the night, sounding barely coherent, but he left a number for Ronnie to call. The staff person awakened Ronnie and she called Matthew immediately. He told her he was at a motel in Portland, Maine and said that if she wanted to see Daniel she would have to come there. Ronnie called Rita, who called Matthew's parents. His father, the police officer, called the Portland police and asked them to apprehend Matthew and hold Daniel until they arrived. Matthew's parents arranged to pick up Ronnie and drive to Portland.

The police picked up Matthew and Daniel. They described the motel room as filthy, with beer and soda cans and fast-food wrappers littering the floor. But Daniel was fed and clothed and watching television, unharmed. Ronnie brought Daniel to Renewal House for a brief time before moving to their new home. Matthew was transferred back to his hometown where he was placed on probation and ordered to get psychological help, one of thousands of Vietnam veterans turning the violence of war into a nightmare at home. Eventually, supervised visits between father and son were allowed with Matthew's parents, who had become very supportive and helpful to Ronnie. Staff members and volunteers helped Ronnie set up her new home and to get on with her life, finally free from violence. Ronnie had made an extraordinary journey from the midst of a terrible war to an entirely new culture and language, to the terrifying experience of violence from one who was supposed to love and care for her. She courageously acted for her well-being and that of her child, building a new life. We were honored to accompany her on part of her journey.

> *The wolf shall live with the lamb, the leopard shall lie down with the kid, and the calf and the fatling together, and a little child shall lead them… They will not hurt or destroy on all my holy mountain; for the earth will be full of the knowledge of the Lord, as the waters cover the sea. (Isaiah 11:6,9)*

The Truth Will Set You Free

There was a growing group of people who traveled with Jesus. They were generally peasants and working people, usually not the rich and powerful, although he had an occasional supporter here as well. All of the disciples had experienced the hardship and compromises of living under the occupation of the Roman Empire. Some had experienced physical abuse, some the trauma of witnessing cruelties such as mass crucifixions or suffering the daily indignities of having to carry soldiers' belongings for two-mile stretches whenever asked. Some had wrestled with demons that told them that whatever hardship they endured was appropriate because they just weren't worth anything. Whenever Jesus would hear such demonic voices, he would remind the people that they were made in the image of the Holy One, as it said in the Torah, "Then God said, let us make humankind in our image." (Genesis 1:26) He would tell them that the negative views of their own worth came from the great Liar, the Father of Lies, as he called the evil one. The truth was that they were beautiful people and to understand that truth would set them free, "...and you will know the truth, and the truth will make you free." (Imagined from John 8:44 and 8:32)

In the New Testament evil is personified as Satan or the devil and is described as the "liar and the father of lies" (John 8:44). One of the greatest of Satan's lies is that some people are simply not worthy. Often people who have been abused physically or psychologically have accepted this lie and believe that they have caused the violence, or that they somehow deserve it. Old patriarchal social ideas reinforce this view.

I once accompanied a woman to get a restraining order after she had suffered repeated abuse and had fled to Casa Myrna. She had left her abusive boyfriend, but he had broken in the door of her new apartment and moved in to begin abusing her again. This time she left with her three children and was hiding in the confidential shelter. I convinced her to get a restraining order against him, but when we got to the court clerk's office the receptionist, on being asked for the proper form, began lecturing the woman. "How can you do this to your husband? Are you taking care of him? Are you thoughtful of his needs? What kind of woman are you to drag him into court?" We had the three small children with us and two began to fuss and cry. I demanded that the receptionist be quiet and give us the form, but it was too late. The woman who was already terrified and confused was now humiliated and was not willing to go forward to get the protection order she deserved.

It is hard to imagine the cruelty and violence that can be present in some intimate relationships. I think of the woman who was brutally beaten by her husband because the kitchen was not clean, but on another day when he found her cleaning the oven, he beat her for not being clean and properly dressed to greet him when he came home from work. (She sought shelter at the Franklin Square Ministry and accompanied me sometimes to preaching engagements, sharing her powerful story and poetry.)

Amarette Calloway, who volunteered with the children at Renewal House, and then served as counselor/advocate, once viewed a woman's particularly extensive bruises, and thought "I am seeing the result of human sin, right in front of me!"

The job of those who minister to abuse victims is often not only to provide practical help but to help them to learn the truth: that they are beautiful, unique, gifted people; that no one has the right to hurt them; and that they are absolutely deserving of safe and peaceful lives. There is nothing more important to see and to affirm in the person who has been abused than this absolute truth.

Sarah was almost immobile with grief when she arrived at the shelter. Her two daughters were in foster care and she was pregnant with a third child. The father of this child had been unable to deal with the idea of a long-term relationship, especially including a child, and he had asked Sarah to leave his apartment where she had been living. She had nowhere to go. At the time she was estranged from her mother, her father had just died, and she could think of no friends who might take her in. Sarah sat up all night in a coffee shop. Finally, in the morning she called her social worker, although she knew it would just further prove what was viewed as her instability and make it harder for her to get her children back. The social worker called Renewal House.

On interviewing Sarah, Rita saw the depth of her despair and arranged an immediate visit with a therapist at a local neighborhood health center. The therapist believed that Sarah was possibly suicidal. She gave Sarah her personal phone numbers and made her promise to call anytime that she felt desperate, day or night. For the first few nights at Renewal House Sarah slept with the shelter phone next to her bed and the nighttime staff person close by.

Rita asked me to come meet Sarah in the role of pastor. She thought that Sarah was suffering multiple griefs and that some special listening and prayer from me would be helpful. I found Sarah lying on her bed in the middle of the day and I sat down beside her. She told me, with little expression in her voice, that she felt almost completely abandoned, but the hardest thing for her was the recent death of her father and her deep, despairing belief that she had caused his heart attack by making him worry over her current difficulties. Sarah had been close to her father, and she told me that he was always the one to defend her and support her and show his affection and love for her. She missed him terribly, but more than that she believed that she had let him down. "His death was my fault. He was so worried for me and upset that his heart just couldn't take it. I broke his heart," she said.

She lay on the bed as she told me this, too depressed to move. I reflected on this with her, assuring her that we almost always feel that way when someone we love dies. I told her that her father had died of a heart attack, not a broken heart. And I prayed with her—for Sarah, for her dad, for gratitude for his time in her life, for forgiveness wherever it was needed. I assured her of God's profound love for her and forgiveness in every moment, and that her father now lived surrounded and held in that love, which wasn't such a bad thing after all. Of course, being held in God's love and forgiveness, her father surely felt only love for her and a desire that she be well and happy. Now he could be present to her in a new, larger way.

At Renewal House, with Rita and others and her exceptional therapist, Sarah quickly got better. When she could accept the loss of her father and grieve without the belief that she had caused his death, her normal brave and feisty attitude came back. As far as her ex-lover was concerned, she said, "Forget the lowlife. He wasn't worthy of me and he doesn't deserve to be a father!" Regarding the custody of the girls, she believed they had been taken unfairly and she would fight to get them back. Her attitude was one of appropriate anger and indignation. She invited the social worker to Renewal House and made a good case that the children would be better off with her there than away from their mother. In the meantime, visitation was arranged for the girls at Renewal House.

Sooner than expected, Sarah's daughters, Suzanne and Mary Lou, were returned to her custody. On one visit Sarah saw a bruise on Mary Lou's arm. The bruise was remarkably shaped like fingers and Mary Lou affirmed that yes, Tom, the foster parent had grabbed her hard. Sarah called the social worker, who responded quickly, and custody was immediately returned to her. Sarah's health and spirit had been renewed; the girls were back with their mother.

Sara's pregnancy progressed and one of the seminary interns became her birth partner, preparing with her and finally accompanying her to the hospital where little Penelope was born. Sara's health and spirits were not only recovered, but she found a new lease on life and put her creative spirit into action. Only one major problem remained for her, and for most of the women who spent time living at shelters: the lack of affordable housing.

Tragically, many women put up with abuse from their partners because this was the price of having an adequate place to live for themselves and their children. Most shelters limit the time that a family can remain. Given Sarah's pregnancy and the birth of Penelope, we continued to extend her time, but with little income she was unable to find a safe adequate apartment for herself and three girls. She decided to do something—she would go public! We helped her to write a press release and find a site for an interview. A news team from one of the Boston television stations came to the press conference and Sarah told her story of living in a shelter for close to a year because of the lack of housing for low-income families in Boston. Public housing developments had long waiting lists and rents continued to escalate in the city. What were families supposed to do? Sarah was featured on the 6 o'clock news speaking up for herself and other women and children in difficult circumstances.

Part of the responsibility of the minister at large is to speak in churches to bring the reality of the conditions of urban parishioners living in poverty to more affluent communities. Since the days of Joseph Tuckerman, the goal has been to establish partnerships to change conditions through public advocacy and other means. While I was at Renewal House, I would often speak in churches about the obstacles faced by abused women. People would often ask, "Why do women stay in a violent home?" I thought that a more appropriate question would be "Why do men beat women?" But the first question is a serious one, and the reasons are multiple and complex, including the fear of what the abuser will do if you leave, not only to you but to those who help you.

And if you do not have a separate, adequate income, and if your family is not able to take you in, what can you do? If you do not have the job skills to earn an adequate income, especially considering the constantly rising cost of housing, what can you do? Now women are able to flee to confidential shelters, but even so, consider whether you would want to live with your children in a shelter with an uncertain future, knowing that you probably cannot afford an adequate, safe home. Affordable housing remains a critically important issue that profoundly affects lives, as do such issues as job training and the minimum wage. You have to be very scared and very brave to flee a violent person and go to a confidential shelter.

Finally, Sarah found an apartment, and after she became settled for a good period of time, we hired her at Renewal House as a part-time staff advocate. From there she went on to work in a variety of social service positions, helping others who felt abandoned and forgotten.

Many years after Sarah had sat alone and abandoned in that coffee shop, fighting the urge to end her life, she became a political advocate for differently abled children and was honored at the Massachusetts State House. She lived a life rooted in the truth of her own value and that of every child of Creation.

Toni was another brave woman who stood up for herself.

She had learned courage as a child, being "baptized by fire" during school desegregation in Boston and its court-ordered busing. Toni was an African American, living in Roxbury, and as a little girl she was sent on a school bus to South Boston, a white working-class neighborhood that was known at that time for its white racism. Boston was on the national news that year as mothers with rosaries paraded in the streets praying and declaring that black children would not go to school in their neighborhoods, and that their own white children wouldn't be bused out. Incredibly, rocks were thrown at the buses filled with students as they arrived in South Boston. Toni had been on one of the buses featured in the news, frightened by the angry faces she saw trying to surround the bus, many of them women; terrified by the sound of the rocks hitting the bus; hustled into South Boston High School surrounded by armed police.

Ten years later, Toni again found herself facing violence directed against her. In college she met and married a foreign student, a man from an African country. Sadly, soon after the marriage her husband became abusive, physically attacking her when she failed to meet his expectations as a wife. After the first beating, Toni went through what many women who are abused go through. She questioned whether it was her fault; she gave her husband the benefit of the doubt that perhaps the circumstances were unusual, and he would never hit her again. She loved him, perhaps she could help him. But after a second beating Toni went to the police.

Now Toni faced violence in a different form. The police filed a criminal complaint, her husband was arrested, and Toni went to court for a probable cause hearing. The judge listened to the story and then asked Toni how she could bring charges against this poor man. Didn't she know how these charges would hurt him? He was obviously a fine man trying to improve himself. Her job was to support him, not bring him to court when he simply lost his temper. The judge dismissed the charges and Toni called the shelter hotline, afraid to return home now that he was released, afraid also to stay with her mother or with friends, believing that her husband was a danger to others as well.

We were appropriately outraged at Renewal House and spent one evening brainstorming how to respond to this judge. Our favorite idea was to have T-shirts made up to say something like "Judge So-and-So Hates Women" or "Judge So-and-So Supports Violence Against Women." Then we would sit in one row of the courthouse and at an appropriate time would all remove our jackets and stand, displaying our message. Instead, we settled for a formal complaint and went to district court, with a different judge, and supported Toni in getting a restraining order. This judge added a vacate order for her husband to leave their apartment. Although the restraining order is just a piece of paper, sometimes it can be very effective, especially in a case like this when the consequences of being arrested would affect a person's immigration status.

Toni was never completely happy that she was unable to pursue criminal charges. Through the many trials of her life, she had come to value herself and recognized the beatings as crimes. She was also humiliated and furious at the treatment she had received from the first judge. That, on top of her childhood experience of violence and hatred, left her with a longing for justice. But life went on and Toni moved on to live a life free of violence.

About twenty years after that first year of Renewal House, I was in South Boston at Carson Beach, another site of racist violence in the 1970s. I lived not far away in Uphams Corner in Dorchester and now often went walking along this Boston Harbor beach and out to Castle Island, site of an old granite fort built in the nineteenth century. On my walks I always made note of people of color, who were still not in great number, but now able to enjoy the walk without fear. I noticed a beautiful woman on one such walk, and suddenly we recognized each other—it was Toni!

She filled me in on the previous twenty years, good ones with all the ups and downs of normal life, violence-free, predominately peaceful. She had never married again but had a long-term relationship and a son who was doing well. Now a single mother, she was living in Roxbury, working and trying to spend as much time as possible painting. She had long wanted to express her artistic soul and recently had been able to spend the time doing so. Toni and I began to meet regularly for walks at the South Boston beach and it was Toni who brought art supplies and ideas to my sixtieth birthday party. Under Toni's leadership we created a large picture of a wild and free and independent woman, a joyful wild woman to be hung on the wall of my condo. Toni was a free soul who lived in the truth of her own unique beauty.

Some of the disciples were pretty well-versed in the scriptures and they would often remind one another of important truths found in the Torah. They were created in all kinds of physical images, genders, sizes, and shapes by the Creator who loved them and wanted peace and goodness for them. They knew that reminding one another of this underlying truth was important in the face of all those social or political forces which would tell them otherwise. As Jesus said, "The truth will make you free."

Friendly Neighborhood Exorcism

Jesus described himself as a good shepherd. He had been speaking to people who were very familiar with sheep and shepherds. People knew that sheep were very dependent on good caretakers. They had many natural enemies and sometimes wandered off by themselves, unwisely. Once Jesus talked about how the shepherd cared for each and every sheep and would search tirelessly for even one sheep who wandered off and got lost. (Imagined from Luke 15:5–6)

The first exorcism I did was in my own building. We were on the third floor of a triple-decker and the tenants on the first floor were experiencing some uncomfortable times. They believed that a ghost or spirit inhabited the apartment, and they were not the first to think so. The previous tenants, two young men, had felt the same creepy sensation at times.

The current residents were a Caribbean family, a mother and two children, and the mother was quite convinced that some soul was inhabiting this space. So, I agreed to try to rid the apartment of the spirit.

Now, I am no expert on exorcism, nor am I well-informed about spirits inhabiting spaces or people. I'm a universalist with both a small and a capital U, and I understand that religious traditions and ultimate conceptions of reality are conveyed through symbols. With the little u I believe that the Holy is present in many traditions, experienced and described in a rich variety of ways. I understand that while many Westerners do not take spirits seriously, people from other cultures often do. I honored the experience of the family.

As a Universalist, capital U, I believe that God desires to save all souls. As I once heard Carl Scovel, then minister at King's Chapel, say in a sermon on Universalism, "God holds the gate open until the last sheep comes home." The good news of Universalism was big on love and God's goodness, if perhaps light on the subject of evil. Certainly, as a Unitarian Universalist, I did not believe in a devil or literal demons.

So, I approached the subject with the idea that if there was a spirit in the apartment that poor soul was trapped there and would much prefer to be freed to journey on and be united with the Holy One. I didn't have a lot of materials on helping souls journey on. The Caribbean family was Christian, and I assumed that any trapped soul in that apartment was Christian as well since the neighborhood had historically been predominately Roman Catholic. Often, three generations of Irish families shared life in apartment buildings like this one that came to be known as triple-deckers—three apartments, one on top of the other.

Not having materials, however, I adapted worship material that I found in the Episcopal Book of Common Prayer. I included prayers that emphasized God's unconditional love, the goodness of Creation, and the power of forgiveness.

I gathered with the family, and we lit a candle to honor the trapped soul. Then I prayed for that soul that had made itself known to residents of the apartment. In as many ways as I could think of, I assured the soul of God's love and power, and God's desire to be united with us all, to bring us home. I prayed that God would offer light for the journey and guide the soul to freedom and to happiness. We concluded the service with the Lord's Prayer and blew out the candle.

My neighbors felt that the service had done its job, that the spirit had traveled home, and they now felt comfortable in the apartment. They were not bothered again. When I shared this story with the staff at Renewal House the counselor, Amarette, said, "Isn't that just like Betty, she even feels sorry for a ghost and tries to help it!"

I was touched by her remark.

Later I was asked to do a spirit cleansing service at the Asian Shelter. My associate minister and good friend, Cheng Imm Tan, had organized the Asian Task Force Against Domestic Violence in the Asian community, and was the force behind the creation of a shelter for Asian women that addressed the cultural and language needs of women from a variety of Asian countries. Cheng Imm was from Malaysia and took spirits quite seriously, so when the guests of the shelter expressed fear and concern that there was an unhappy spirit in the house, she felt a service would be called for.

It was through Cheng Imm that I came to have a special attraction and love for Kwan Yin, the Chinese goddess of compassion, "she who hears the cries of the world." Who would be more concerned for any restless soul than this bodhisattva who, when you approach her for prayer, has tears in her eyes because she is so happy to see you? The residents and staff of the shelter joined me in praying to Kwan Yin to assist any unhappy souls to travel to a place of peace. Again, things quieted down, although this spirit seems to have returned later and we had to do a repeat ceremony. I wonder how Jesus exorcised so many demons. They saw him, I think, and they just felt that they were loved. They either had to accept that love or leave. Some of them were afraid and left; others just ceased to be demons.

Sheep were important animals, in spite of their limitations. The shepherd cared for them in the face of any danger and would rejoice over any one of them that was lost and then found. When he finds a lost sheep, the shepherd lays it on his shoulders and rejoices. And when he comes home, he calls together his friends and neighbors, saying to them, "Rejoice with me for I have found my sheep that was lost." (Imagined from Luke 15:3-6)

COMMUNITY

> With our imagination as well as our eyes, that is to say like artists, we must see not just their faces, but the life behind and within their faces. Here it is love that is the frame we see them in.
>
> *Frederick Buechner*

A New Marriage, a New Church

For I am about to create new heavens and a new earth; the former things shall not be remembered or come to mind. But be glad and rejoice forever in what I am creating. (Isaiah 65:17–18)

I was honored and excited to be the co-chair of the newly organized Urban Church Coalition, along with the Rev. David Eaton, senior minister at All Souls Church in Washington, D.C. Organized at the 1979 UU General Assembly, the coalition members were ready to make future Assemblies aware of the issues of urban justice, poverty, racism, violence, and the importance of the often-abandoned urban churches.

We held an open gathering the first night of the 1980 General Assembly in Albuquerque, New Mexico, to introduce our concerns. I was aware of a young African American pastor raising relevant and prophetic questions and statements. I learned that he was Graylan Hagler and that he was a Christian Church (Disciples of Christ) minister serving a Unitarian Universalist church in Chicago. I looked for him at the Coalitions' hospitality suite later that evening hoping to recruit him and found that he was clearly looking for me. That began an unexpected romance in Albuquerque.

Graylan had a rental car and in between Urban Church Coalition meetings, events, and strategizing, as well as other obligations, we explored the surrounding area together. I was surprised that this Black Disciples of Christ minister, from Baltimore, currently serving a UU church in Chicago, seemed to know all the country music songs playing on the car radio. He told me that he had pastored a church in Utah one summer and enjoyed the music. To say the least, Utah had been an interesting experience for this eastern African American pastor.

We drove into the hills surrounding the city and stopped at a little tavern, where we sat at the bar and ordered a drink. Suddenly, Graylan stopped talking to me, quickly finished his drink, and abruptly suggested that we leave. I felt his withdrawal and was a little hurt and confused. I was not particularly aware of the white men at the bar who apparently were not pleased to have an interracial couple in their midst. I definitely learned through the following years to be aware of these racist attitudes, understanding that people of color live their entire lives with a sensitivity to their environment that most white people can only imagine. It was a useful introduction.

By the end of the week, it was clear that the relationship had developed into something serious, something that we both wanted to explore further. Graylan drove me to the airport, and we made plans along the way for him to visit me. By the fall he had moved to Boston. That September a new era opened in both our lives and in the fall of 1981, we became Ellis-Hagler.

In true activist style, Graylan began going to community meetings and became particularly involved with education issues, where he found dedicated organizers. At the time he was driving a cab for income but very visible as a clergyman in social justice movements. Seeking a minister, education advocate Hattie McKinnis approached Graylan with sad news. Her grandchild had died of sudden infant death syndrome. Would he perform the funeral? Of course, he officiated at the service.

And that was the beginning of the Church of the United Community. Hattie and her daughter, Lois Stroud, the mother of the infant, asked Graylan if he would consider starting a church. They believed that there was no congregation in the city that was radically inclusive and had justice as a primary theme. They sought a congregation whose minister was on the front line, outspoken for people who needed a voice. In response to this request, we held a gathering in our third-floor apartment on Darling Street in Mission Hill. Graylan and I led a worship service there, followed by lunch and a productive organizing discussion. We were African American, Latino, White; we were welfare advocates, education advocates, former Renewal House guests, gay and straight, young and old.

"What were people looking for?" we asked. And people responded: a church that was inclusive of race and culture, where you wouldn't be judged, and it didn't matter what you wore or how you looked. They wanted a compassionate church where all could express their feelings; a church on the front line of social justice issues; a church with a prophetic liberation theology; a church of united communities.

Graylan was the organizing pastor, and I was co-pastor. The ministry at large allowed for this, and I led worship or preached as I was able, given that some Sundays I preached at the Urban Ministry's member churches. The Urban Ministry's executive director, Bud Murdock, offered us space in the building in Park Square that housed its administrative offices as well as several other nonprofit organizations. Later the Christian Church (Disciples of Christ) became interested in the project. After visiting us, their outreach director, Rev. John Foulkes, insisted that we leave the downtown location and move into a diverse neighborhood, and awarded us an organizing grant enabling us to do so. Later, the Unitarian Universalist Association and the United Church of Christ joined The Christian Church (Disciples Christ) in supporting the Church of the United Community. I was privileged during those years to be given ordained status with the Disciples.

Graylan arranged to rent a building called, at the time, the Marcus Garvey Center. A three-story building in Roxbury, a block from the First Church in Roxbury, it had been a symbol of black empowerment at one time. It was then taken over by Rastafarians, and ultimately was shut down when it became a center for illegal drug activity. There was a large picture of civil rights activist Marcus Garvey on the side of the building. We rented the building, but later in a dispute with the landlord, Graylan discovered that they didn't own it. The city owned the property, so we sought and received permission to continue using the building. From the perspective of the city, this building, which was once a site of drug dealing, was now becoming a church and center of service to the community.

By that time, Graylan was serving a multi-staff downtown church in a part-time position, so the Church of the United Community could not meet until afternoon. This was perfect for me on the days that I was preaching because I often had no time during the week to prepare, and so Sunday morning would be writing time. It was also my first regular use of the Christian church lectionary, which we followed. It became a spiritual discipline to give myself over to the scripture and write. I would be amazed sometimes at the movement of the Spirit on those days. I would start out feeling that I had nothing to write, only to discover inspiring texts with layers of meaning and possibility.

One of the church's first decisions after moving was to agree that Narcotics Anonymous could use the space for a daily noon meeting. This was a large and popular meeting and many of the regular members began to come to church. Soon the congregation had a sizeable population of people in recovery from drug addiction, and as the church leadership was organized it included many from this community. There were also a regular number of social activists who became part of the church, as well as a few seminarians. We were a diverse group expressing the united community vision well, and under Graylan's prophetic leadership continued to advocate for justice and provide a voice for those who were voiceless.

The worship service of the United Community developed a unique style, including traditions from the three sponsoring denominations, all of which were governed by congregational polity and respected local church autonomy. We often recited a poem by liberation theologian Dorothee Sölle as a statement of faith. Our communal prayer always included a prayer for the "poor and suffering addict." As lay leadership developed from the recovering community we were often led in a shouted praise of God in as many languages and images as people could imagine. "Praise God! Alaba a Dios! Praise Allah! Praise Mother God! Praise Father God!" and continuing with the images that came to mind.

One ritual that was central to the Disciples tradition was weekly Communion. Our Communion was open to all people of all ages and was a moving remembrance of Jesus and of the presence of Christ in each of us and in community. We would gather in a circle to pass the bread from one to another and often a child would follow with the cup of juice (rather than wine in respect for people in recovery) Sometimes there would be a song that would come forth spontaneously following the communion and would last as long as the Spirit moved us.

I was privileged to participate there until I was called as the senior minister at large and executive director of the Ben Frat, which precluded my serving in any one particular congregation. But I consider the Church of the United Community significant in my growth as a Christian, or "Jesus follower" as I often called myself then, and for a while it was a true spiritual home. Graylan was eventually called to serve the Plymouth Congregational United Church of Christ in Washington, D.C. and, in spite of an extension grant from the UUA, the Church of the United Community did not endure long without his unique leadership. However, the old Marcus Garvey building became a harm reduction center, helping addicts to live and to get clean.

> *"I will rejoice in Jerusalem and delight in my people… No more shall there be in it an infant that lives but a few days, or an old person who does not live out a lifetime… They shall build houses and inhabit them; they shall plant vineyards and eat their fruit… They shall not labor in vain or bear children for calamity; for they shall be offspring blessed by the Lord." (Isaiah 65:19–23)*

The Annunciation: Yes, I Will!

Mary of Nazareth was visited by an angel who surprised her with a rather astonishing proposal. The angel asked if Mary would be willing to bear God's child. Mary was a young girl and not at all sure what this might involve. As she pondered this remarkable request she had a range of feelings; certainly there was some fear and some confusion, but the idea of being filled with God, and then bringing life and divinity into the world, was enormously exciting to her. She thought about it and then, "Yes," she said. "Yes, let it be with me just as you say." Mary said yes, and so the holy was born into the world. (Imagined from Luke 1:26–38)

My friend and I were on South Street in Philadelphia one evening, heading for the falafel place. There was a man on the street collecting money in a can with a sign saying that the collection went to fight cancer. I stopped to put something in the can and spoke with the man. He showed me, unasked, an "ID" from an American Baptist Church. Maybe it was authentic. Maybe the handmade sign was authentic, and the money went to an anti-cancer fund. I had no way of knowing. By the man's appearance it would not have surprised me if he was homeless and collecting money for himself. It didn't matter to me. "Give to everyone who begs from you," Jesus said, and I've found that to be a lot easier than trying to judge everyone's truthfulness or intentions under these circumstances. On the other hand, I do listen to Jesus's advice about being wise as a serpent while innocent as a dove. It's a hard balance to maintain!

My friend told the man that she was recovering from cancer. He offered a nice prayer and said "Amen," and then I started to pray for him. He seemed surprised. Not five feet from us people were dining outside at a nice restaurant on a beautiful evening. I like this kind of thing, meeting someone briefly and praying for one another on a street corner amidst lots of human activity. Such times remind me of Michael.

Kip Tiernan, the founder of Rosie's Place, a homeless shelter for women in Boston, and respected advocate for the homeless, would often say, "You stand with the crucified or the crucifier." Michael, having experienced some amount of crucifixion in own his life, made a clear choice as he created his ministry to the homeless.

Michael was a very slight man. A good-looking man, he was quite clearly and openly gay, and clearly and proudly clergy, always sporting light-colored clergy shirts with a clerical collar. He and his partner Tom lived in the South End of Boston with their two terriers. I met Michael in the early days of the Church of the United Community.

One of the founding members of the church always referred to it in the plural, the "united communities," because its small numbers included so many different identifiable groups and the issues they represented. So, when this 45-year-old white gay man came to be in fellowship with us, the congregation welcomed him warmly. Michael was affiliated with the Christian Church (Disciples of Christ). He had received his Master of Divinity degree and fulfilled most requirements for the ministry but was not yet ordained.

The process of ordination in a congregationally organized denomination requires that a candidate for ministry be recognized and called by a local church. The issue of LGBTQ clergy had been very controversial in the Disciples movement at that time, with some churches affirming and some strongly and vocally opposed. Michael needed to have his own calling seen and affirmed for his ordination to move forward. And the ministry to which he felt called was unconventional: he wanted to minister to the homeless.

Michael's plan was to raise money to support a street

ministry in which he would befriend homeless people wherever they were, wherever he met them. He would be their pastor, in the way of the minister at large, and would respond to their needs in a pastoral way. He would listen to them, pray with them, eat with them, laugh with them. Working with shelters and outreach programs, he would advocate for their well-being. Michael was clear: it was the whole person with whom he was concerned, that unique and wonderful individual created by God. Michael saw the face of God in each homeless person.

Michael joined the ministry team of United Community. We were an interesting collection of mostly unpaid ministry staff who met weekly. Graylan was an outspoken social activist, Gospel-driven in his concern for the poor and the oppressed and his desire to challenge empires; Greg was a Quaker and developing a community-based economic ministry; Tony was a formerly Pentecostal Puerto Rican preacher from Spanish Harlem; Dr. Dbinga was an exiled clergyman from Zaire (now the Democratic Republic of Congo); and I. All of us—two African Americans, an African, a Puerto Rican, and two white Americans (one woman, one gay man)—met to contribute to the creation of this new congregation with its united community.

Michael participated fully in the church, which was not always easy. There is no necessary separation between activism and social service, but there can be a tension between putting your energy into changing the system and providing hands-on care for the wounded of society. Ideally, ministry includes both—that is certainly basic to the idea of the ministry at large envisioned by Joseph Tuckerman. But it is hard to maintain that balance and people need to follow the path of their particular gifts. Michael understood himself as a pastoral street minister and although he was challenged around the issues of activism, he held his own. He stood in support of those social activists working on behalf of housing and homeless issues, as well as gay issues, but his ministry was on the streets as a pastoral presence. He would see and affirm the presence of God in these others, as he needed to be seen himself in wholeness and truth. Further, he considered his life itself the activism; he was an openly gay man with a sacred calling, which he would follow despite the multiple hurdles he had faced through the years. Michael had heard an invitation which he understood as a calling from the Spirit, and Michael had said yes. He would be who he was. "Yes," Michael said. "Yes."

The congregation witnessed Michael's commitment and voted enthusiastically to ordain and officially call him to a ministry for the homeless. The ordination service was held at the First Church in Roxbury, the oldest wood-frame church building in Boston, now part of the UU Urban Ministry. Historically, this is the site from which William Dawes left to ride to Lexington to warn the revolutionaries that the British were coming. (Paul Revere is only more famous because of Longfellow's poem.) In this present revolutionary situation, the regional minister of the Disciples of Christ came from New York City to participate, to bless, and to preach the sermon. In addition to the congregation, the service was attended by a large number of gay community members who had been through the long journey with Michael. When it came to laying on of hands, the whole community was invited to participate. The lightweight Michael could barely maintain his kneeling position under the weight of all who wanted to add their affirmation and blessings. His partner Tom and others openly wept. It had been a long road for Michael, but he felt called by God to ordination and he had fought for it.

Many people are afraid of homeless people. Some who are without homes have mental health or addiction issues. As a small, openly gay man, Michael was vulnerable to attack, but I never heard him express a concern. He was welcomed by people on the street as someone—a religious figure, a pastor—who cared about them.

One day Michael asked if we could meet for lunch. We met in a little cafeteria in Brigham Circle. How nice it was, I thought, to have informal time with Michael. This nice occasion with Michael took a shocking turn, however. As we launched into our salads, Michael told me that he had AIDS. It was the beginning of this horrendous epidemic in which people in the gay community as well as IV drug users were contracting the disease, unknowingly, and dying with horrible speed.

Michael asked me to be his spiritual director in the journey into this time of what was, for him and for the gay community, a true plague. Over the next few months Michael's condition declined quickly. He was no longer able to leave the house and I would visit him on Sundays and take Communion to him. Weekly Communion is a tradition of the Disciples and we had created a very personal, informal, and powerful inclusive service at the church. I hoped that this would bring him comfort in the midst of his rapidly deteriorating health. Together we would say the Words of Institution, remembering Jesus at the Last Supper, remembering the solidarity of Christ with those who are suffering, aware of crucifixion, hoping for the resurrection. Michael grew weaker and weaker, and I did what I could through listening and prayer, but Michael and Tom's friends in the gay community were the true pastors and spiritual mentors and companions. A community of people who were suddenly losing lovers and friends and neighbors to this devastating virus surrounded Michael and the others with their loving presence and care.

The memorial service for Michael was held at the First

Church in Roxbury in the Quaker style of silence, with people speaking from the silence and in the Spirit. I understand that there was much testimony among the many open tears. I was in Connecticut attending a regional Disciples conference and I had been asked to lead a brief memorial service for him there. It was a difficult choice, but I believed that Michael had fought for his standing and recognition within the formal church. The region included some congregations where the leadership was vocally anti-gay. But in the brief memorial service at the conference, we remembered and affirmed the Reverend Michael Schloff, minister to the homeless. A revolutionary figure in his own right, Reverend Michael paved the way for many others.

Mary listened to angels and the Christ was born into human life. She was brave enough to open her heart and mind as the Spirit spoke to her and to believe in amazing possibilities. Michael too listened to the voice of the Spirit calling him to ordained ministry as an openly gay man in an unconventional ministry; calling him to stand with the abused and the poor on the street or wherever he found them; calling him to love in the face of society's denials, and to bravely stand in the love of his partner, his neighbor, and God. Michael said yes and the Holy was born into the world.

A Journal Entry from 1983

Jesus came home to Nazareth after being baptized and then tempted in the desert. He had done a little preaching on his way home, but this was going to be the big moment to begin his mission. He was nervous about how the people of his hometown would respond as he called them to help in the building of the Kingdom. He decided that he would remind them of God's call to create justice. There were no better words than those of Isaiah, he thought. He would quote Isaiah! Should he read about "repairing the breach, being a restorer of streets to live in?" Yes, that would be good, but even better: "The Spirit of the Lord is upon me, because he has appointed me to bring good news to the poor, He has sent me to proclaim release to the captives, and recovery of sight to the blind, to let the oppressed go free."(Imagined from Luke 4:16-18; Isaiah 56:12b)

I love living in the city, but some days it's hard. A picture of Christ crucified hangs on my bulletin board. The picture, clipped out of a magazine, shows an alley, buildings, trash barrels; a small piece of sky shows slightly through the wires and apartment buildings. Jesus hangs there in an old loading doorway, alone, forgotten, crucified in an alley of the city.

The picture remains central to my wall, surrounded by pictures of loved ones. There are my parents, my partner, a picture of Lee and Rachel when little, playing in a bathtub. There are quotations from the Bible and other sources that have moved me. A letter confirming my certification for ministry is there. And Jesus, the Christ, hangs crucified in the center, in the city.

The other night we picked up Rachel, now 15, and a friend downtown. She had gone with friends to a North End restaurant, walked with them through city hall plaza, playing at imitating statues and various historical figures. They had ended up on the back of Beacon Hill at a friend's house for hot chocolate, where we picked them up to come home.

Driving up our street we noticed a car stopped and some young people running away. We stopped to see if we could help. A man stepped out of his car angrily raving about slashed tires and how he would blow the motherfuckers away. "Oh my God" said Rachel, looking at the gun in his hand. A foot from the car, gesturing angrily, the man held a gun, determined to use it on the tire slashers.

Jesus hangs in a doorway, in an alley, on my street. As I make my way down the hill, past trash cans, past dogs, past the burned-out building, the old deserted cars, the vacant lot owned by the slumlord, the paved rental parking lot owned by another slumlord, Jesus hangs there ...deserted in the vacant lot, wounded in the burned building, broken in the abandoned car. Jesus. Christ. Knifed in the alley, mugged on the street, shot, destroyed by heroin. Jesus, with us in solidarity, with us here, with us in our sorrows and rages, proclaiming presence with us, unending love and hope for us, and the promise of resurrection, here in our lives in the city.

I was called down to the shelter for an emergency. Someone was sure that another resident had a gun. On my way, the leader of the daycare next door to the shelter stopped me. She said that they had been getting cockroaches and they must be from the women's shelter next door. Of course, where else would cockroaches come from but poor women, forced to flee their homes. I arrived at the shelter and the woman in question invited me to search her things, which I did, and I didn't find a gun. Not this time. I hope never. Jesus Christ, son of God, savior, have mercy on us, sinners.

Jesus did not receive a very good response to his first sermon! In fact the people ran him out of town. What was all this about being sent to the poor and the oppressed? The people wanted some happy benefit of having a prophet in their midst! But Jesus was committed to bring God's promise of peace and justice to the poor and the broken, even to the point of suffering with them. And it would not be an easy way to go.

Any Excuse for a Party

There were certainly challenges for us followers of Jesus of Nazareth. We traveled the countryside and worked hard supporting him in his ministry of teaching and healing and feeding people. But one thing about Jesus, he loved a good party. We not only enjoyed the hospitality of humble people who shared their bread and fish, but we were sometimes invited to feast at the homes of wealthy people. Zacchaeus, for example. He was a wealthy tax collector and, being a man short in stature, had actually climbed a tree to get a better look at Jesus. Jesus called out to him and invited himself and the rest of us to his house for dinner, where we were wined and dined in style. While the work of following this teacher could be exhausting, we were so often rewarded by gathering for a meal with stories and laughter. (Imagined from Luke 19:1–6)

I was forty and I was not feeling happy on my birthday. For one thing, my father had died the previous December and I missed him. It was the first of forty birthdays that I didn't have a dad. For another thing, my partner was not willing to celebrate it with me. I had a regular evening staff meeting scheduled at Renewal House but I had decided to skip it so we could go out to dinner or for a drink. And Graylan suddenly became all work-centered and suggested that since he had to go to a meeting I should too. Weren't people depending on me? Wasn't it important that as the director I should be there?

That made me angry on top of depressed. Who was he to decide what I should do? Who was he to make any kind of judgment about my participation in my own ministry? I told him what I thought. I saw a look of bewilderment on Graylan's face, but for some reason he further urged me to go to the staff meeting at Renewal House. I got madder, more indignant.

Finally, Graylan sighed. "Okay," he said, "I don't know

what to do but to tell you. They're having a surprise party for you." Oh. I felt sheepish and sorry that I hadn't caught on. But, of course, I felt warmed by the knowledge that others had been thinking of me and planning this event. So, I went to Renewal House, ready to be surprised.

"Surprise!" They all shouted as I walked in the door. The guests, staff, and many of the volunteers had gathered to decorate the living room. The children, too, had prepared with homemade birthday cards for me, smiling proudly as they presented them. There was a gift and there was a cake and ice cream, of course. And for an evening we all could forget our problems, our losses, and our worries, and enjoy a good party.

Renewal House was like that. For an environment where several women were in serious life crisis, victims of domestic violence and consequently homeless, and where there were children who had fled with their mothers, often terrified by violence in their homes, there certainly was a lot of generosity and a lot of laughter.

There were many parties at Renewal House: birthdays, housing-find celebrations, obscure holidays. "Any excuse for a party," we sometimes said. These parties were often a "loaves and fishes" kind of experience, for there would suddenly be an abundance of delicious food and treats for the kids. Volunteers and especially some of the ministerial interns that regularly staffed the shelter would often provide various forms of engagement and entertainment. My good friend and colleague through many years, Cheng Imm Tan, was a particularly energetic and creative staff person. She would bring her wok and teach cooking one evening, and the next evening would lead the guests in a class of aerobic exercise.

As mentioned before, Cheng Imm later became the associate minister at large and director of Renewal House. She organized the citywide Asian Task Force Against Domestic Violence and a shelter for Asian women. Eventually the mayor of Boston recruited her to organize and become the first director of the Office of New Bostonians, an outreach program for the city's immigrant population.

The experience of ministering in a shelter, like all social justice activities, has many sad, infuriating, and frustrating days since so many obstacles arise to make things harder for the guests to move forward. And there are tragedies—women going back to men who will hurt them again, unable to find housing or feeling lonely and discouraged. But it is a mistake to think that doing such work is primarily depressing. When a group of people get together to help one another there can be a joy that transcends most other experiences. The beauty and the hope and creativity of the human spirit shine through the difficulties. The community becomes a healing source not just for the wounded, but for the helpers, too. It becomes, if even briefly, a beloved community, inspiring and sustaining all who are there together to make a new and better world.

A card came to Renewal House once, inscribed with the words that we used for a motto sometimes. "Each day with hope we greet the rising sun. We battled death with laughter and laughter won."

We saw some very sad things when we followed Jesus. We saw increasing conflict and we witnessed the oppression and hardship with which people lived under the occupation. But we were sustained and encouraged by one another, by the love of the community that developed among us, by the meals with one another, the parties, and by the laughter.

An Interconnected Web

Jesus had a preference for poor and working people, which he made pretty clear from his first words in this hometown, "I have come to preach good news to the poor..." and by calling fishermen as his first disciples. One day he drove a rich man almost to tears, telling him that he must give away all that he had in order to see the Realm of God. The man was very wealthy, and just could not see his way to doing that and went away very depressed. But this was not the whole story, . On the one hand, Jesus made clear that with God all things were possible, and he had some well to do friends, like Nicodemus. On the other hand, he did point out that it would be easier for a camel to go through the eye of a needle than for a rich person to enter into the kingdom of heaven. Jesus was talking about fairness, about equity, about a fair distribution of resources. God made the world and its plenty for everyone. He challenged us to figure out how to see that equity was accomplished "on earth, as in heaven." (Imagined from Luke 4:18; Matthew 19:21-26, John 19:39, Matthew 6:10)

It always seemed to snow on Sundays! I grew up in Seattle, Washington and snow was a rare occurrence, but now I was here in Boston where people actually considered it a normal thing, and even drove in it! And it always seemed to snow when I would be scheduled to drive to some suburban church to deliver a sermon. This was part of the responsibility of the minster at large at the UUUM, to carry the word of the reality of poverty in Boston to more affluent communities, and to make connections to change and to improve things. So, in the face of the scary weather I would get in my car and venture onward, rain, snow, or sleet! Sometimes this required loud and vocal prayer as I drove. (In New England they do not cancel church due to snow!)

At the time that I was there the UU Urban Ministry had 60 member churches in the Boston metro area. Churches had three delegates and elected the board of directors at an annual meeting. Some congregations sought to do more, to find direct connections to our programs, and to work with us on issues of social change. And many of them regularly invited the ministers at large to speak.

Preaching in the suburbs was always interesting and sometimes moving. I loved writing the sermons and preaching them, but it was a challenge. How to bring the reality of poverty and violence to affluent congregations in a way that was truthful and could be heard and would motivate people? How to bring this truth to people without making them feel unnecessarily guilty or ashamed, but to acknowledge our interconnectedness and responsibility? How to acknowledge our common humanity, including suffering, and at the same time point out that their suffering was done in the comfort of secure homes and economic comfort and easy access to services.

I told stories. For example, I wrote and delivered three different sermons about Diane, the woman murdered by her husband. Of course, writing helped me to deal with that terrible reality. I wrote many sermons about the young men incarcerated and shot, as well as women and children who fled violence only to be left unable to afford a home. I wrote about courage, and creativity, and love. I framed the stories in Unitarian Universalist principles, especially the inherent worth and dignity of every person; a world of justice, equity, and compassion; the interdependent web of existence of which we are a part.

Sometimes I would be met with polite good wishes, but no future involvement. I remember one occasion when no one spoke to me at coffee hour. I just kind of stood there by myself with cup in hand, no one venturing my way, looking for a way to get out of there gracefully and quickly. A member of that church contacted me a week or so later to say that some members had actually met to brainstorm ways they might help, and they would like to put on a Christmas party for Renewal House families, and then follow up with families to help in other ways. They stood ready to put on Valentine parties, Easter parties, and so on, with gifts and treats for all, especially focused on the children. They did a wonderful job and were appreciated! It was clear that I couldn't always tell what touched and moved people when I visited and preached!

Other churches helped in other ways. There was the annual Rock for Renewal House fundraiser at the First Parish in Bedford; (I still have the t-shirt and canvas bag!) There was help organizing and participating in a Roxbury church workday, in which crews of people worked on the grounds of those three acres, and had people sponsor them to raise money; there were many volunteers for special projects, and professionals who offered pro bono services to people in our programs.

At one of our annual meetings at the Roxbury church, the minister from the First Church in Bedford, John Gibbons, suggested the possibility of an urban-suburban legislative group of some kind. I gathered a few people to meet over this idea, including the Holy Spirit group (Thomas Mikelson, Scotty McLennan, Anita Farber Robertson) with whom I met for spiritual sharing, John and a few other ministers who had expressed interest. I invited my friend Margaret Blood as a speaker. Margaret had worked as a staff person for a state legislator, and then created and directed an advocacy group focused on legislation to create universal preschool education in the Commonwealth of Massachusetts (a goal which they succeeded in accomplishing!). Margaret gave a dynamic presentation on the power of citizen organizing. She said that one letter to a community newspaper concerning a state legislator was worth more than a thousand-dollar donation. She pointed out how powerful we could be because we came from so many different legislative districts, many of them affluent. Legislators in some of these districts rarely, if ever, heard from constituents on issues arising from poverty in cities. We could make a difference!

Thomas Mikelson proposed that we hire a lobbyist! He suggested that we find ways to raise the money, and he immediately pledged $500 himself, challenging all to find ways to contribute. There was enthusiastic agreement (although some might have gasped a little quietly) and the Tuckerman Coalition was born, appropriately named after the UU Urban Ministry's founder, Joseph Tuckerman.

Margaret recommended Lisa Simonetti for our lobbyist, with whom we were very pleased. As her first activity, Lisa arranged an early morning gathering with the legislators from the various districts that we represented. We all showed up at the Massachusetts State House expecting one or two legislators to actually make it—but—we could hardly fit into the room that Lisa had reserved because all of our reps were there! Lisa introduced the Tuckerman Coalition, but then nobody knew what to say at first, so I suggested a prayer, which I offered. This was quite appropriate of course because we were a coalition of clergy, even if Unitarian Universalist, and it gave us a moment. Then we shared our particular concerns about legislation directed toward issues affecting low-income people in cities. The legislators were aware, of course, that clergy represented whole congregations in their districts as well as often having a broader impact in their communities.

Lisa continued to educate us to relevant efforts at appropriate legislation. One in which we joined with many other advocacy groups was a bill which would provide for every young single mother to have an older mentor from the community, who would regularly visit and assist her in learning how to care for her child and how to access services that would help them. We were happy to see that bill pass. Eventually, my colleagues from the United Church of Christ City Mission Society and United Methodist Urban Ministry joined the coalition and we met for several years.

In the 1830s, Joseph Tuckerman was completely clear that urban poverty was everyone's responsibility, and that the Ministry at Large was serving both rich and poor. He tried to create a model in which rich and poor would work together to eliminate poverty, with particular responsibility for those who had the power to change systems so that poverty would be eliminated. He didn't use the word systems in those days, but that is what he spoke about – laws, education, institutions, neighborhoods. Today, the ministers at large continue to live and minister in poor communities, working with others to respond to the needs of the time, and continue to seek ways to enlist the active, transforming help of more affluent communities to create a more just society.

The lessons that Jesus taught were not necessarily easy ones. While he made clear that God's immeasurable love was for every person, he expected those persons who had more to share with those who had less. He expected those who had talents to use them and share them; he expected generosity. Once he told a parable that upset many of the disciples. It was about a landowner who hired people to work, and paid them all the same, even after some of them had come later than others. Those who had worked the longest were understandably angry, but the landowner chided them for their lack of generosity. What did they know or understand about why the people came late. And when all was said and done, all the people had to eat, their children fed, and clothed. (Imagined from Matthew 20:1-16)

Church of the United Community and the Gerasene Demoniac

Jesus traveled around a lot from place to place. He felt the need to spread his message about the presence of God's reign, God's love, and the need for the people to love one another. He wanted to share the good news and along the way to do some healing, some feeding, and to drive out a few demons. So, he traveled from place to place and one day he arrived at the land of the Gerasenes, where just stepping off the boat he was greeted by a distraught, naked, and truly crazed man who threw himself at Jesus's feet. There seemed to be multiple voices coming out of the man's mouth, as if an army of demons possessed him. Jesus got down on his knees and embraced the man and ordered the demons to leave him. The naked man relaxed in his arms, peaceful for the first time in years. Jesus asked people to help the man to be clothed and rehabilitated and warned him that life would not necessarily be easy as a demon-free person, but life would be filled with love and hope, and that would be worth staying free of them. (Imagined from Mark 5:1–20)

Part One: Tony

Tony Ruiz had been, in his words, "saved" in Spanish Harlem by an ecumenical outreach program there. He meant that he was saved in two ways, first from heroin and its deadly addiction, and saved from sin by the good news of the Gospel. He became a preacher in Harlem and was ordained somewhere along the way by an independent church. He had just arrived in Boston and had checked into the Narcotics Anonymous meeting at the Marcus Garvey building in Roxbury. When he learned of the new Church of the United Community there he joined eagerly and became one of the volunteer ministers on the clergy team.

Tony often acted as a right-hand man to Graylan, attending many of the meetings with the three denominations interested in supporting the church. On one occasion, he attended a gathering at the Beacon Hill headquarters of the Unitarian Universalist Association. Tony was new to UUism and was taken aback when he quoted the Bible to make a point and one of the participants told him that Unitarians did not consider the Bible as authority or even necessarily believe in God. The group was surprised when the Puerto Rican street minister from Harlem responded by quoting Saadi, a medieval Persian, "I fear God and next to God I mostly fear them that fear him not."

Tony Ruiz was a brilliant and charming addition to the church and ministry team; he had an inclusive and friendly nature and a sense of humor and enjoyment of life. In the first weeks and months Tony helped with the church in every way possible. Unknown to us, however, Tony was not fully in recovery! He may not have been using drugs during that time, but he was not doing the constant, hard, internal work involved in true recovery. As someone said to me about alcoholism, "It's not a drinking disease, it's a thinking disease."

Graylan and I were going out of town, and we were expecting a COD delivery of some equipment for a radio show we were planning. Tony offered to cover the office so Graylan gave him a check for the amount of the equipment but did not specify the recipient since he didn't know to whom it should be made out. Tony cashed the check and disappeared.

When Tony returned to the neighborhood a few days later Graylan was waiting. I'm told that he chased Tony up and down the street and told him that he had two choices: "Go into a residential recovery program, or die." Tony chose recovery and entered First Academy, an excellent yearlong residential program. The program is difficult, and many people drop out, but the success rate for those who stay is high. I missed Tony during that year, but when he came out, he returned to our community and continued as an extremely valued member of the church as well as a friend.

Tony was brutally honest about his days as an addict. For example, he told me that one day when he was feeling desperate for drugs he went home and cleared out all the best clothes from his wife's closet, which he then sold for drug money. Tony laughed, sharing this brutally honest picture of himself, saying, "How low can you get?" This, he said, was what crack in particular did to people. And, of course, stealing from the church was not something he was proud of either. But now, truly in recovery, Tony worked hard to make up for the pain he had caused others and to be of generous service. Tony was diabetic and ultimately had to regularly undergo dialysis. He died a few years later, greatly admired and loved.

Tony Ruiz was a true minister. His compassion, his humor, his acceptance and enjoyment of other people, and his deep sense of calling from a higher power made him an exceptional pastoral presence to others. How devastating it was, then, to consider the years he lost, and the pain caused to those who loved him by the destructive power of addictive drugs. Tony redeemed himself through his sobriety and service to God and others. Countless other lives continue to be destroyed by addictive drugs. Today, headlines announce a new and worsening drug crisis, this time involving opioids, often leading to heroin, and sometimes laced with an even more powerful synthetic drug called fentanyl.

When community prayers were offered at the Church of the United Community there was always a call for help for the "poor and suffering addict." This is a prayer for those who are addicted, for all whose lives they impact, and for the whole community, which not only experiences the destruction caused by addictive drugs but misses out on the gifts of those whose lives are destroyed. If we consider that we are one body of humankind, then we must recognize that this body is wounded, that we are wounded. Such prayers, along with concrete actions, are needed as much today as they were then.

Part Two: George

When I led worship at the church, I sometimes felt like I was a television program rather than a live, embodied version of myself. I would be preaching what I thought was a pretty good, engaging sermon—at least I was engaged—and I would be getting into it with feeling, hoping for a few "amens" or "yeses," and suddenly a man in the front row of the congregation would get up and walk out of the room. It didn't feel like he was angry at me, just kind of like I wasn't there at all. Before the end of the sermon, he would be back sitting where he was before, the fragrance of cigarettes wafting my way. Someone in the middle of the room, too, might just as suddenly get up and walk out, again returning in a few minutes. This was especially common after George started bringing people from the Boston City Hospital detox to Sunday morning services.

I wasn't offended by this, though I found it appropriately humbling. Those men and women from the detox center had a lot more on their minds than being courteous to the preacher, and I knew that their ability to sit still was sometimes limited, as well as their ability to go for long without a cigarette. I valued their presence at the church, and I was grateful to George for bringing them.

George Kenney was an active member and lay leader of the church. He often recounted how he was able to recover from years on the street as a drug addict. As he told it, he had been in and out of detoxes and in and out of drug programs and he knew all the answers and all the ways to outsmart the counselors. Consequently, he defeated himself and always went back on drugs. One day, however, George was in the old Charles Street Jail, one of many brief incarcerations, and there all of a sudden, he met Jesus. He didn't really understand it himself; he'd been in many churches and been preached to a thousand times. But there was Jesus with him in the Charles Street Jail. It was a presence that he could feel, as surely as if he could see and touch it. In the midst of his detoxing, in a cold cell, sick as a dog, George knew that God was there for him in the person of Jesus. In his mind he saw Jesus clearly and it was as real to him as anything had ever been in his life. George knew suddenly and inexplicably that he was not alone, that someone was holding him, suffering with him. For the first time he felt something entirely new, something he had never felt during the nightmare of his addiction. George felt that he was being offered hope, a way out of the real prison of his addiction. There was something better than drugs, there was, as he described it, a "pearl of great price!"

George was a strong presence in the church and in the recovery community, sponsoring countless other men and providing inspiration to many in and out of the recovery community. While his own religious experience centered on Jesus, he was very inclusive in welcoming all to the church. Each Sunday he led the congregation in shouts of praise to the "God of your understanding": Praise God, Allah, Yahweh, Higher Power, and so on. The old Marcus Garvey Center rocked with enthusiastic shouts of praise.

In the midst of the AIDS plague, George went to be tested. The whole congregation prayed fervently, and I think believed that his test would be negative because of the power of George's faith and vision. There was a general sense of shock and despair therefore when George tested positive. One could feel the whole church fall into a kind of depression after George shared the news, which he was not resigned to or at all humble in receiving. No, George was very angry. He was angry especially at God and he let it be known. He believed that he had been faithful in responding to God's call to be clean and sober, to stay clean and to use the power of his example and his personality to help other addicts. It hadn't been easy. In addition, he had joined the church and was active in bringing other people in; he had met Jesus, and he shared the experience. He prayed. He had asked for what he wanted, in Jesus' name - he wanted to get a negative HIV test; he had promised God that he would continue to do the work of God and help others. God had let him down.

It would have been easy for George to go back on drugs at that point. What did he have to lose, after all? If he was going to die of AIDS, he might as well feel good doing it. But George knew that he had everything to lose; he had that "pearl of great price" that Jesus talks about; he had the one thing that mattered; he had his own soul, his sobriety, his true self, that spirit within that was somehow, despite it all, at one with God. He didn't understand with his mind. He felt betrayed in his understanding, but with the "eyes of the heart," in his gut, he knew that God's presence was with him still and he chose to be faithful.

George continued in his role in the church and his leadership in the recovery community, and that doorway of hope for a meaningful life stayed open. George responded well to the drug cocktail that they were just trying out at that time and had many more years to lead and inspire.

It wasn't easy for the man in Gerasene. The army of demons was gone but now he had to take the normal responsibility of being human and living each day choosing life and goodness and justice and service. It wasn't easy for Tony or George to remain clean and sober. Being clean meant having to look at oneself and the years in which those drug demons were in charge of one's life and soul, and that takes incredible courage. We are all flawed, wounded human beings, challenged to look at our demons in one way or another. These two "grateful recovering addicts" were able to do that and to direct their lives to helping others and building a healthy community. They turned their lives over daily to that Higher Power, and God and the community loved them into wholeness, and they in turn loved others, defeating a legion of demons.

Good Friday March

On that evening before his death Jesus gathered with his close friends and followers. He took a basin of water and a cloth and got down on his knees before each of them. Gently, he took their feet into his hands and washed them, one by one, men and women, each disciple. He remembered how Mary of Bethany had done the same for him a few days before. Mary had recognized that the powers were organized against Jesus and in all likelihood he would die. She wanted to honor him with her gift of sacred oil, to recognize not his death, but the power of his life. Jesus looked around the room at that last upper and he too, before he left them, wanted to honor the beauty and the power of each of the lives in that room. He wanted to share with them, in his wisdom, the most important thing in life. As he touched each of them he paused, looked at them directly, and said, "You say that I am your leader and teacher. If I who am your leader and teacher can wash your feet, you ought also to wash one another's feet. As I have loved you, you also must love one another."

That evening Jesus was arrested and tried by a religious court. The next day he was turned over to the Roman governor, ridiculed, betrayed, and crucified. (Imagined from John 12 and 13)

It was Good Friday and members of the Church of the United Community gathered at a housing development in the Mattapan neighborhood of Boston to walk the Stations of the Cross. This ancient Christian ritual recreates Jesus's last day as he is condemned and walks the path to the cross on which he is crucified. There are various stops, or stations, along the way to remember the event in detail, including moments when Jesus stumbles and falls, his interaction with the women who mourn for him, and a meeting with his mother. The ritual continues through the crucifixion and ends where Jesus is taken down from the cross.

Those church members who were familiar with the ritual explained it to those for whom it was a new experience. We were to imagine that we walked the path that Jesus walked, but in our own time. We would remember Jesus, but we would also remember those who had died unnecessarily and brutally in our time—honoring the unique beauty and wonder of each life; mourning unnecessary and violent death; pledging ourselves, in solidarity with Jesus, to love one another by changing the conditions around us that led to violence.

Jesus lived under the reign of the Roman Empire, which established and maintained its peace through violent oppression and military might. For example, near the town where Jesus had grown up, two thousand people had been crucified at once for an insurrection against the Empire. Now we were living in a democracy and the violence that we protested was another kind of violence, the violence of inequality, poverty, and racism, which killed many thousands of people. Daily it took the lives of young people and others through the trade of illegal and deadly drugs, and through the proliferation of guns in communities where families lived. In this context we were followers of Jesus, and we were trying to do as he had instructed us, to love one another. We remembered and honored those lost by pledging to save those still among us.

"This has to end! We have to take our community back! Get the drug dealers off the corners!" yelled John as we stopped at different sites along the way, corners where drugs were sold, streets where there had been death from overdoses and lives destroyed by guns. John was a leader that day, loud and clear and ready to confront the evil that had taken over neighborhoods. He was a new member of the church and only recently in recovery from years of drug addiction. He was a small, thin man and the years of drugs and street life had left their mark. Now he saw an opportunity for renewed life, for rebirth as someone clean and sober.

John understood that his own sobriety was tied up in helping others to get clean. He especially wanted to help young people to stay away from drugs, and to get the drug dealers off the streets. He was impassioned that Good Friday, as he joined church members to walk the Stations of the Cross. He loudly denounced the sins that crucified Jesus and the sins that continued to crucify people in the community. He challenged others to join in the effort to protect our young people.

As we walked, we remembered Jesus. We remembered that he stumbled and that he fell, and we pledged to help those among us when they stumble or fall. We remembered the stranger, Simon of Cyrene, who stopped to help Jesus carry the bar of his cross, and we hoped that we would stop to help the stranger. We remembered the women who mourned and his mother who grieved, and we asked for God's help to see and to comfort the grieving ones among us; we remembered the unnamed woman who wiped Jesus's scratched and wounded face with a damp cloth; and we called for the crowd to gently touch and comfort and heal one another. We recalled how Jesus had washed the feet of his followers the night before the crucifixion and then instructed them in the way of discipleship. "Love one another," he told us, "Love one another."

John continued to be an impassioned spokesperson as we proceeded through the housing development. "Take back the streets. Stop the violence." In addition to church members walking, there were members of the recovery community, and increasingly neighbors joined us. We had been asked to walk the Stations of the Cross in that particular neighborhood by a church member who lived there. She had especially wanted us to make a show of solidarity and support for the mother of a young person recently shot to death by the police. So after a few stops at corners, we arrived at the home of Betty Johnson.

There, Betty and a group of neighborhood women greeted us. We stopped and prayed, and we remembered Jesus at the crucifixion. We remembered, with sorrow and with anger, the beautiful life and the tragic death of Betty's son, Donald.

Donald had been shot to death by police after taking a joyride in a Greyhound bus. A friend who worked at a Greyhound station had given him a key to a bus to take out for a spin. It wasn't the first time, and of course Donald always brought the bus back—what would he do with a Greyhound bus, after all?

This time, however, someone discovered it and reported the bus stolen. The police caught sight of it and tried to pull Donald over, but he was scared and made a bad judgment. He decided to run instead. The route he followed as the police pursued him indicated that Donald was on his way to his mother's house. Donald was scared and trying to run home.

The police chased the bus into some narrow backstreets of Jamaica Plain, a residential neighborhood of Boston, and there they managed to stop and surround the bus and then to shoot Donald, who was unarmed and trapped. He died from a bullet to his chest.

We stopped at Donald's mother's house, and we remembered those last days of Jesus' life and we tried to remember the gentleness and love in which Jesus held each of his disciples. We tried to remember what he said as we reached out to Betty and remembered Donald. "Love one another as I have loved you," Jesus said. Love one another.

Donald was bold and a bit reckless perhaps, but certainly not a bad kid. A shelf in his mother's house holds the certificates and awards that Donald earned growing up. One of them was an award that he had been given by the mayor when he was fifteen for rescuing people from a fire. Donald saw a building in flames and while some people just stood and stared, he ran in, leading a mother and three children to safety.

Nobody knows exactly why Donald was driving the bus that night. His mother said that he was a dreamer with a love of buses and travel. "Why didn't the police just follow him?" she asked. "He was coming home. I would have talked him out of the bus and he would be alive."

Betty walked with the crowd, wailing, as Mary must have wailed when Jesus died—two mothers whose children had been brutally and unnecessarily killed. The other neighborhood women walked with her, their arms around her, touching and loving her in her grief. Betty was a brokenhearted and brave woman who protested all the way to the mayor and let the public and the community know that her son was a good child. She had come to the church for support in her efforts to hold the police responsible and to clear the name of her only child. We had helped to press for a special investigation, but in the end the shooting was called justified.

So, we walked the stations of the cross remembering Jesus, remembering those who had died from drug addiction, or gun violence, or from the continuing effects of racism. "Hold the police accountable!" yelled John. "Take back our streets. Protect our youth!" The women from the neighborhood supported Betty as we walked. Sometimes we sang as we walked: "Where were you when they crucified my Lord . . . where were you when they crucified my son, my daughter, my mother, my father . . .?" We remembered the crucified on that walk, those who died from drugs, those who died from violence—intended lives, beautiful unique people whom Jesus had asked us to love.

John did very well in his recovery from addiction. He combined his now active church membership and his attention to his recovery with social activism. He reached out particularly to young people, trying to get them away from drugs and the street that could take their lives. But the Good Friday march was the last event in which he would be able to participate. John discovered that he had AIDS and became very ill. This was early in the epidemic and although the new drug cocktail worked for some patients, more widespread treatments had not yet been developed. Countless recovering addicts were finding that they recovered from drug addiction and the pain that went with it, only to experience the heartbreak of AIDS. The virus spread to John's brain and his condition deteriorated quickly.

One sad Sunday George, many years before his own death from the virus, told the congregation of John's death the night before. In his last days, George and others from the community were by his side. John was in considerable pain and the doctors wanted to give him pain medication, but George told us that John refused. "I am a grateful recovering addict," he said. "I have been living clean and I will die clean!" The people around him tried to tell him that this was not the same as using street drugs, this was medical treatment for the pain of the disease and there was no harm in using it. But John insisted. He had found life and his true self, and he would not give that up for anything. And so John died as a "grateful recovering addict" clean and sober. His friends gathered around him, and they washed his arms, his legs, his feet. "Love one another," Jesus said. Touch one another. Hold one another. Love one another.

Once there was a brave young man who ran into burning houses to save others and who loved buses. Once there was a small, thin older man who knew the joy of sobriety after years of drug addiction, who found purpose and relationship in the last year of his life and refused pain medication so that he could die clean. Once there was a mother whose only son was unnecessarily and violently killed, but who refused to be quiet about it and confronted the establishment loudly and repeatedly.

Each of these was precious to the Creator, wounded by the struggles of life and the social sins of the world. All were intended for full lives, some dying before their time. All gave to life more than they had received. They were born into poor neighborhoods, falling into temptations that awaited them from their earliest days, being good some days and stumbling others, struggling to recover from the falls and to live a good life and help others. Each had a unique personality, a way of smiling, a way of laughing, ideas, relationships. Each of them was loved imperfectly by the people in their lives, and profoundly loved by their Creator.

On the night before he was crucified, Jesus met with his disciples. We were an imperfect group to say the least. Each one of us had our successes in life, but also our failures. We had our strengths, but also our fears. Each of us had stumbled in life, and all of us had loved. Jesus got down on his knees before every one of us to hold and to wash our feet. We were all there and it was hard because we knew that we did not deserve to be so touched and loved. And then he told us what we were to do – we were to receive that unconditional love and then we were to love one another in the same way. We knew that we would probably fail at that many times, over and over, but we were to continually get up and try again, (Imagined from John 13:4–11)

A First Silent Retreat

Therefore, I will now allure her, and bring her into the wilderness, and speak tenderly to her. From there I will give her her vineyards, and make the Valley of Achor a door of hope. There she shall respond as in the days of her youth... I will make for you a covenant on that day with the wild animals, the birds of the air, and the creeping things of the ground; and I will abolish the bow, the sword, and war from the land; and I will make you lie down in safety. (Hosea 2:14,15,18)

"This is my commandment, that you love one another as I have loved you." (Jesus in John 15:12)

It was my first spiritual retreat, and it was raining. I had looked forward to leaving the city for some meadows and woods and I had signed up for a weekend retreat at the Jesuit Campion Renewal Center in Weston, Massachusetts. I had been seeing George Drury, SJ, for a few months for spiritual direction, and he had suggested that I take the next step and try a silent, directed retreat. I had met with George the previous evening and now on Saturday, following George's instructions, I had planned to try some walking prayer or contemplation, meditating on scripture and praying as I walked. But now it was raining!

Well, the rain wasn't that hard, and I had a raincoat, so I decided to do my walking prayer in spite of the rain. I copied the scripture that George had suggested for prayer and put it in my pocket and headed off to the meadow. The scripture reading was from the book of the prophet Hosea, an appropriate passage about being called into the wilderness for reconciliation and renewal. Here was a flowering meadow and a grove of trees next to it, just as I had hoped for, but I thought grumpily, "How can I enjoy them when it is all so wet?" I was disappointed. Nevertheless, I tried to pray the scripture as I walked, even as the ink on my paper started to run down the page. I tried to open my heart to God, to ask for God's grace, as George had suggested, as I slowly said the words of the scripture: "It is for this that I have lured you into the wilderness…it is for this…to return your vineyards…to turn the valley of Achor [meaning a place of trouble] into a doorway of hope." I repeated words and lines from the passage as I walked, staying with phrases or words that seemed to touch my spirit.

Gradually, through the silence and the scripture, through the effort to open my heart to the Spirit, I became aware of some of the deeper feelings that I had brought with me to this retreat. In the quiet meadow, images and memories rose to the surface and I became aware that walking there in the rainy, woodsy place, I was, underneath it all, very angry. Enraged, really. This was not long after John had died and all of those wrongly ordered sufferings and deaths were very present to me. Diane, Michael, Donald, John, Corrine, Laura—just a sampling of the violence and death and failure of love all around me. The addicts who couldn't make it and went back to drugs, or got clean and died from AIDS; the abused women who tried to leave but couldn't find affordable housing, or couldn't believe in a violence-free life and went back to brutality; the neglected and abused children deprived of all the safety and resources they deserved; the mentally ill in state mental facilities, or on the street, without adequate care or attention or love. My heart was filled with the abandoned, the helpless, the victims from these first years of ministry. I felt the grief of this, and I was angry because it was all so wrongly ordered, unjust, unloving, wrong. And I was so powerless, so helpless in the face of it.

Here I am in a lovely retreat center trying to open myself to the Holy—whatever that is, whatever that means—but what kind of God are we talking about here? What kind of

God allows all this suffering to happen? Why do I want to have anything to do with such a God? What am I doing here?

I tried again to pray the scripture as I walked, and the wind began to pick up. The rustling of the trees sounded so much like my name being called. The earth, the wilderness, seemed to hold me. I looked up at the big stone building in the distance and the cross on top, and suddenly I saw the crucifix in my imagination. But it wasn't Jesus on the cross that I saw, it was Melody—a young friend, as she had once described herself—in the emergency room during a psychotic episode, stretched out, tied down, in terror. And then there was John dying of AIDS on the cross, and then Diane, and then there were multiple scenes of crucifixion. There were the women, bruised in body and spirit, the children abandoned, the young men shot.

And where was God in all this crucifixion, I wondered. *Where was God?!!*

And then I realized, of course, a crucifix, of course, God was on the cross with us. I saw that God was right in the middle of it all in the person of Jesus, the face of God, the embodiment of God, the symbol of God, Jesus, was in the middle of all those places, in all those scenes. It was the Jesus of the Gospels suffering with the people, loving us without condition, challenging the powers that would injure and oppress, and calling us to love one another in the same way.

I saw Jesus with the battered child, holding her, weeping with her; and there was Jesus with the woman who didn't believe herself worthy of a life free from violence, and he was embracing her with a powerful love. I saw Jesus in my imagination in solidarity with the others, loving them, crying with them, comforting them. And then I saw that this incarnation of the Holy was angry, too—about John, about Diane, about Peggy, about the victims of violence, about the abandoned and unloved, angry about the disorder of sin. This beloved of God came among us to show us the path of steadfast love, the way of forgiveness and peace, and we weren't getting it, and Jesus was grieving and angry too. Where was God? God was with us.

My eye was drawn again to the cross on top of the massive old building—the empty cross. Yes, there was the crucifixion and there was resurrection. There was death and suffering, but there was life and hope. In the Christian story God suffers with us and continuously offers us new life, another chance, and commands us to love one another. In that great Universalist spirit, it is the God who will not give up on any single one of us. I saw God's despair and anger at the suffering, so much deeper and more powerful than mine could ever be. And her continuous offering of another chance to get it right. "Love one another," she instructs us. "Love one another!"

And the wind continued to rustle the leaves, sounding so much like my name. I prayed the words, "It is for this that I have lured you into the wilderness, I want to return your vineyards, turn the valley of Achor into a doorway of hope." I wept. God wanted to give me back my vineyards. I had no particular association with vineyards, but I understood that I had lost something and the whole point of the spiritual life was to find it again.

> *"I will make for you a covenant on that day with the wild animals, the birds of the air, and the creeping things of the ground; and I will abolish the bow, the sword, and war from the land; and I will make you like down in safety…and you shall know the Lord." (Hosea 2:18, 20b)*

DISCIPLESHIP

> My prayers for a world without violence are constant. I pray for courage to take risks, for a humane spirit, and for the healing of us all affected by violence.
>
> *Deborah Prothrow-Stith and Howard R. Spivak*

What Can I Do to Help the Poor?

When Jesus spoke to crowds, he usually included special blessings for people who were poor. "Blessed are you who are poor" he said, "for yours is the kingdom of God" Sometimes it was the "poor in spirit" but always those who were poor had a central place in Jesus's life and mission. He had begun his ministry, of course, by quoting that famous line from Isaiah, "He has anointed me to bring good news to the poor." (Imagined from Luke 4:18)

I had become restless in my role as associate minister at large. Renewal House was thriving, which was good in terms of institutional health, and sad in terms of the need for a domestic violence shelter. I loved the Church of the United Community, but it was primarily Graylan's ministry, and it was a parish after all, and I still felt the call outside of the organized church. I was involved with interfaith groups and neighborhood groups that addressed issues, but that was a part of any ministry that I would do. I was restless in spirit and wanted something new. Then in 1986 Ben Frat's senior minister and executive director, Bud Murdock, announced his intention to retire.

As soon as the announcement was made people urged me

to apply. I could not imagine being the executive director. Bud's favorite opening line in many meetings was, "It's a good thing I was a banker before I became a minister." Bud had overseen a partnership with the US Department of Housing and Urban Development and local community groups to build low-income housing in Roxbury. It had been a complicated project that needed his particular skills. In more recent years Bud had revived the ministry at large and overseen such things as the merger of the First Church in Roxbury into the Ben Frat, a very important ministry, but one that I saw as almost entirely administrative. No, thank you, that was not where I understood my gifts to lie.

I understood myself as a liberation theologian, directly involved with people, with issues concerning people on the margins. On the street, not in an office. I found energy and joy, if sometimes heartbreak, in being with people in their struggles.

People continued to encourage me, however, including my friend and mentor Jack Mendelsohn and my good friends and colleagues Scotty McLennan and Vic Carpenter. Jack thought that I had a good chance to be called to the position if I just avoided things like being arrested during the search period (for civil disobedience, of course). At General Assembly, the annual continental gathering of Unitarian Universalists, people I barely knew encouraged me to apply and one younger colleague even gave me some fashion advice! (I guess the denim skirts and T-shirts didn't have the appropriate executive look.) Others, however, suggested that I was just too radical to be hired. I could certainly not get along with the Republican National Committee member who was board president, they said.

An interim minister was hired for a two-year period and a search committee was formed, so there was no hurry for me to decide. During the first year the opportunity came to participate in a two-week trip to El Salvador and Nicaragua. We would travel with Dorothee Sölle, a liberation theologian, and bear witness to the violence and injustices there that our government was then supporting. I signed on for that life-transforming experience.

In El Salvador there was a revolutionary war being waged against the US-supported right-wing government and its death squads. In Nicaragua, the Contras, a counterrevolutionary movement supported by the United States, were trying to undermine a popular people's revolution. For two weeks we traveled in those countries and met and heard from a variety of people including priests, theologians, nuns, and ministers. We heard tragic stories and met incredibly brave people, such as the "Mothers of the Disappeared" in El Salvador. We met with a Lutheran pastor at his home while a military helicopter hovered overhead. We worshiped with Christian base communities, the heart of liberation theology in action. We did all of this while meeting and reflecting with Dorothee Sölle.

Surprisingly, it was in Managua at the National Assembly that I suddenly had the information that I needed to discern my own calling at that moment of my life. We met with a legislator from a rural area of Nicaragua. He was a farmer and landowner who explained that before and during the revolution he had been involved in a local Bible study group. Following Vatican II, such groups had been springing up all over Latin America; nuns, brothers, and priests took to heart the message that people should be taught to read the Bible for themselves. They went in large numbers to be engaged with people in poor communities to study the Gospel message. Over and over, people in El Salvador and Nicaragua told us this story—that when people read the Bible for themselves they saw two important things that they had not understood before: that Jesus preferred the company of the poor—he hung around with them, loved them, and sought their well-being; and that God desired the people's freedom from tyranny and hunger and oppression. The Jesus of the Gospel stood with the people in their desire to be free. The Latin American bishops, too, stood in solidarity with the oppressed and said that God had "a preferential option for the poor."

The legislator said that he had been part of such a Bible study group. He saw that God sought freedom from poverty and servitude for the poor, and decided to divide up his land and give most of it to the people who worked it. When the National Assembly was formed in Managua after the revolution, he was asked to represent his district. He said that he did not want to leave the beautiful countryside and that he did not like the city. He was a farmer, he said, and loved the land. He had an education and management experience, and he knew that he was the best qualified to do the job. So he asked himself, "What can I best do to help the poor?" That was his criterion for making such a major life decision.

The question stayed with me. What can I best do to help people who are poor? The legal, historical mission of the Ben Frat was to provide ministers at large to the poor of the city. The focus of the agency was "the poor" of Boston; the resources, the energy, the attention of this old venerable Boston institution existed to help people who were economically and socially marginalized and disadvantaged. Although we struggled for the politically correct language, the purpose of the Ben Frat was to assist in eliminating poverty through the means of the ministry at large—it was to help people who were poor.

I understood this mission, and in my heart and spirit I understood and was faithful to it. I was not the only one able to do the job, as was the case with the Nicaraguan legislator.

There were certainly plenty of competent ministers. But I understood the mission in my heart, and I was there at that time with a sense of calling to the vision, if not to management. And how could I best help "the poor?" By leaving the Ben Frat and going somewhere else to minister, for I was definitely at a transitional point? By remaining an associate and looking for new ways to fulfill the mission under someone else's leadership? Or by being in a position to promote the vision, the understanding, the theology, the history, and the potential of this truly amazing ministry at large?

I understood this mission; I felt called to articulate and lead it. Certainly, I would be giving up the freedom of the associate's position and taking on some administrative work that did not necessarily appeal to me. But after all, what could I then, at that moment in my life, do better to help marginalized people? And what a privilege and honor it would be to lead this unique and wonderful institution.

God has had a wonderful way of putting the right paths before me in ways that are so clear, so stark, that I could not miss them, and still I hesitated. I came to a turning point in the ministry, nine years in and things changed, and I didn't know whether to stay or go. People were telling me that I should be the director. I couldn't see that, and so God led me to Central America, where people were literally dying for their faith and I heard from one of these truly brave ones, "I had to ask myself, how can I best serve the poor?"

I couldn't join the revolution in Nicaragua or El Salvador. I had family, I didn't speak Spanish, and it was not my community or culture or history. But there I was in an institution in my own city that was looking for leadership, and even if I didn't quite know how, I was a leader, I was smart, I could learn, and God placed this before me and had to shove a little for me to see the way.

So I went home, and I told Rhys Williams, the chair of the search committee, that I would apply to be the senior minister at large and executive director of the Benevolent Fraternity of Unitarian Churches. (And by the way, Dan Needham, that Republican board chair, and I became a great team and good friends! Dan was not only a brilliant lawyer, but a committed, compassionate humanist who gave his time freely to help others.)

Some of Jesus's most controversial teaching was included in a talk that he gave sitting on a big rock on the side of a mountain (although some claimed that it had been given at another time down on the plain). He said that the poor were blessed, which was a little hard to believe, but he said that they would inherit the kingdom of God. Jesus told people to be merciful, to love their enemies, not to judge, and to give to all who asked of them. It was pretty radical, but not surprising that Jesus said these things if one thinks about it, for he himself usually hung out with people who were poor, and they were truly blessed by his presence.

(Imagined from Matthew 5; Luke 6)

Seek the Reign of God First, Part Two

> *"Therefore do not worry, saying, 'What will we eat?' or 'What will we drink?' or 'What will we wear?' For it is the Gentiles who strive for all these things; and indeed, your heavenly Father knows that you need all these things. But strive first for the reign of God and God's righteousness, and all these things will be given to you as well." (Jesus, in Matthew 6:31–33)*

I sat in my office in Park Square in Boston. Wow. I was now the executive director of this wonderful old Unitarian ministry to low-income neighborhoods of Boston. I decorated my office with considerable thought. On the wall I hung a painting of two Native American women on horses. It was called The Guardians. I considered them symbolic of protective spirits, or angels for a difficult assignment. I had a Bible on a stand in the corner under a small bulletin board with appropriate inspirational sayings. And now I needed both the guardians and the Bible! I was preparing to face the auditors for the first time for an annual review, along with the treasurer and board president. I was immersed in trying to understand a multi-page report on fund balance accounting and to be clear on such things as realized and unrealized total return.

A level of panic arose in my being. I don't understand this! Under the watchful eye of the guardians, I took a breath and saw the Bible. I turned to the Sermon on the Mount and there in the middle were words to guide my journey: "Strive first for the kingdom of God and God's righteousness, and all these things will be given to you." As hard as it was for me in my panicked state, I stopped and prayed—just for five minutes—but I stopped and prayed, and then I returned to fund balance accounting and learned what I needed to know. Eventually, I even had fun with budgets and accounting. They were like a giant puzzle to solve: How to get the income one needed to do the work one dreamed of? (One of my first decisions as director was to hire a development director to raise money.) And spreadsheets . . . let's see . . . if I put this here, what will happen there? It was a welcome occasional balance to the face-to-face, often crisis-dominated ministry.

I had been overwhelmed and anxious, trying to learn something that was entirely new to me, and I was guided to stop what I was doing, take a deep breath, and pray. This is the heart of the spiritual life. To seek the kingdom of God first with faith and trust. To seek that reign of the Good first, to alter and organize and order one's life to the Good. The word order comes from the same root word as "ordain," the Latin *ordinare*, to put in order, to arrange. To seek the kingdom first is to order one's life to the right order of Ultimate Good. And that means keeping in mind that life is dynamic and constantly changing and so, for one to be faithful, it calls for continuing and constant prayer and discernment. Even in five-minute doses. As Joseph Tetlow, SJ, puts it, "God creates us momently."

> *"Therefore do not worry, saying, 'What shall we eat?' or 'What shall we drink?... But strive first for the reign of God and all of these things will be given you as well."*

A Baby Is Born

They weren't the best circumstances in which to give birth to a child. Mary and Joseph had traveled from the north, from Galilee, all the way to Bethlehem because of one more unreasonable demand of the occupying Romans. They were required to register their names in their place of birth by a certain date even though Mary was very pregnant, expecting her first child any day. When they arrived in Bethlehem they found that the inns were all full with other travelers, at least the ones they could afford. One innkeeper, seeing Mary's condition, had compassion for them and allowed them to stay in the shelter where his animals were kept. He gave them an old blanket and suggested that they pile up straw under it for a bed for the pregnant girl, for Mary was almost a child herself.

Mary and Joseph were not to have any rest that night. As soon as they had settled down on the straw Mary had her first labor pain. Joseph, feeling a bit of panic, ran into the street to call for a midwife. The word spread almost instantly, and two or three women came running to assist Mary with the birth. As Joseph waited outside, he heard the cries of his young wife as she struggled to give birth, but then there was quiet, and then another cry. This was not Mary. Now he thought he heard Mary laughing. No, this cry was that of a baby. Yes, a baby was born! A baby!

Mary held her newborn child with feelings of complete wonder and joy. Here was a perfect little person, with all of his fingers and all of his toes. He was looking right into her eyes, squinting really, as he seemed to be trying to take in this new adventure of his life. Mary loved him enormously, instantly. Life was transformed for her. Her baby was born. A child was given her. Joseph came in and saw the miracle of this new child and he too laughed with joy. That old barn seemed to be filled with bright light and it felt to Mary and Joseph that they were surrounded by a host of celestial beings as they wrapped the little baby in bands of cloth that the women had provided. What would the life of this new little child be like? (Imagined from Luke 2:1–7)

Damien Funderburg's funeral was held at a Baptist church in the South End. His tragic shooting death was added to a number of recent such events, alternating by neighborhood in a cycle of violence and retaliation. Graylan gave the sermon and issued a challenge to Damien's friends, who huddled together in black hoods on the balcony: "Don't retaliate! It's destroying communities as well as individuals. You have the power to stop it! Stop the violence! Honor your friend, Damien, by living, not dying. You have lives to live!! Don't retaliate!"

It was my first glimpse of the young people as a group. They called themselves the Blackhawk gang and had loosely organized in response to other gangs invading their turf. They were being exploited by older drug dealers using their streetcorner services. Damien had been a positive force among them, a charismatic young man who had enthusiastically responded to efforts by our staff to find positive alternatives to gang activities. The gang did not like Graylan's challenge and they stood up, seeming to act as one unit, and walked out, hunched over, hoods up, feigning anger, while grieved and probably terrified. Their leader, beloved and hopeful Damien, had been shot to death.

Rubina Qureshi, our staff person at the First Church in Roxbury, had spent the previous four years making connections in the community and welcoming neighborhood groups into the church. Although the First Church had a beautiful, historic sanctuary that could seat a thousand people, in the 1970s the congregation had dwindled to a handful of white parishioners, most of whom had moved from the now largely African American neighborhood. A decision had been made in the 1970s to merge the property into the Benevolent Fraternity, (now going by the name of Unitarian Universalist Urban Ministry) which would offer programs and services to the community. Since that time, it had been the site of a variety of activities aimed particularly at youth.

Through Rubina's efforts we established an afterschool program in partnership with another historic institution, the Thompson Island Education Center. In the nineteenth century, with Joseph Tuckerman's involvement, the Thompson Academy was established as a farm school for delinquent youth on an island in Boston Harbor. In recent years the school had become an Outward Bound summer and weekend program for inner-city youth. We partnered with their staff for an afterschool program at the church parish hall for middle school youth, who also attended weekend programs on the island.

Rubina knew that a Boston foundation was offering grants to hire gang outreach workers, and acted quickly. Soon we were interviewing for the position, and hired Jerry (not his actual name), who had been active as a volunteer that summer, trying to find activities to keep the youth busy during those violent times. He immediately and strongly urged us to bring the gang into the church parish hall. As a first step, Jerry—who had been there himself at one time in his life, dealing drugs and spending time in prison—convinced the youth to put down the gang colors. They got Damien killed—there would be no more Blackhawks gang.

I took the proposal to the board of directors. This was not without risk. There had recently been a shooting in a Roxbury church during a funeral. There was no respect for any institution. This was the 1990s; the times were crazy, and people were out of control. The directors agreed unanimously that we should, in the words of the newly organized Ten Point Coalition, "adopt" the gang and welcome the members off the streets into the historic old First Church in Roxbury. The Ten Point Coalition was organized by a group of clergy concerned with the violence that had broken out among black and Latino youth. They proposed ten strategies for directly involving people and institutions in responding. One of the first points included having churches "adopt" their local gang, mobilizing the resources of the church community in partnership with other agencies and organizations, creating working relationships wherever possible to respond to the crisis in the community. They developed a model of partnerships and programming that is highly respected nationwide.

So, the former Blackhawk gang members, grieving their loss and frightened of the future, came into the church. Of course, there were rules established right away. Rubina and Jerry held a session with the young people to negotiate and establish rules that they all agreed to. No hoods up. No profanity. No guns anywhere near the property. And if you had another weapon you had to give it to Jerry when you came in and he would return it when you left.

The youth came every weekday and stayed from after school through the dinner hour, with the program providing dinner. These were the most dangerous hours for the young people and the first priority was to get them off the street. Jerry was aided in his new position by several volunteers, many of them from the Narcotics Anonymous community, seeking to put their sobriety into helping the youth of their community. One of the most faithful volunteers was Damien's mother, Queen Funderburg, who turned her grief into tirelessly helping the other youth. On the first Thanksgiving following Damien's death she invited all the youth to her home for dinner. Later Queen became the childcare director at Renewal House.

Probably because of the Narcotics Anonymous involvement, each evening ended with the young people and adults circling up for a moment of quiet prayer, perhaps the serenity prayer, or some word of inspiration. It was an incongruous moment and very touching to me, as the youthful innocence of these young people showed briefly in their faces. These young men and women were trying so hard to be mean and tough and safe in a world not of their own making and stacked against them.

And it was certainly a new experience for me. Although I had participated actively in the community, my ministry was with adults and those actively seeking help and support. Now I was the director of the agency responsible for the Roxbury church and what went on there, and I was confronted with a group of adolescent urban gang members in a time of crisis in the community. I knew full well that some of these young people might just shoot someone if the situation required it, or maybe had already shot someone. I could see that they were unique and beautiful people, young reflections of divinity. Yes. Deserving to grow up fully, to live productively. Absolutely. And realistically, some of them under the right circumstances, could possibly be violent.

Sometime during those first weeks I had a dream. I was in the church office and a young person—or was there more than one?—moved aggressively toward me with a threatening look and I, though frightened, said, "You cannot hurt me. I am protected by God!" And the person backed off immediately. "Thank you, God," I said later, "for the reassurance."

The program flourished as more volunteers came forward to help create activities. An international conflict resolution group from Cambridge volunteered to create and run a program. Minister at Large Peter Thoms, who was a lawyer and minister, started a children's law project, educating young people about the law. Poets Ted Thomas Jr. and Susan Roberts led a poetry workshop and produced a beautiful anthology of the young people's poetry. Minister at Large Cheng Imm Tan organized a job preparation program for the youth, and our board and volunteers found a few summer jobs for the participants.

Through the years I came to know some of the youth. I met Jason in the first weeks of the program. At Jerry's urging we bought a pool table to lure the gang into the parish hall and I saw Jason playing pool with a large knife sticking out of his belt. I asked him for it and he gave me a hostile look, reminding me of the rule, so I got Jerry and Jason gave him the knife. During that first year Jason was shot in the buttock. It was not a life-threatening injury and it was safer to leave the bullet where it was, so he wore it like a badge of honor. After his recovery Jason became a friendly and positive force in the group and, after completing the job prep course that Cheng Imm had organized, spent most of the summer at a large law firm in one of the jobs our supporters had created. Jason was a bright and likeable young man and was doing well there until, unfortunately, he flirted inappropriately with one of the woman lawyers and was terminated early. He learned many lessons that summer. Jason went on to college and did well.

I was often called upon in the clergy role for young people who got into trouble. There was Carl who had a hard time giving up street life and I visited him several times in the local Suffolk County House of Correction. It was a good jail to visit. The guards respected the clergy and always gave me a Bible and a private room when I came in. Carl was interested in the Bible studies and conversations that we had. I also visited him in the hospital after he was shot and wounded. Carl had seen the shooter get ready to shoot him, but in those few seconds he was aware that there were children playing immediately behind him. He knew that if he moved out of the way the bullet would likely hit one of the children. Carl did not move.

There were these young people and many others who used

the opportunity of a safe space and caring adults to get on with lives that would be safe and productive. There were other lives, like Damien's, that would be lost senselessly, tragically. Every one of those young people was created in the image of the Sacred and intended for full, rich, joyful lives.

The labor pains came on suddenly that evening in Roxbury. Gloria was sixteen and pregnant and had no idea what to expect. She was scared. The father of the baby, also a teenager, had long since removed himself from the picture. Gloria's mother, still a young woman herself, called a taxi and the two women set off for the hospital. Kind people whisked Gloria up to the maternity wing where other women waited through the labor pains, expectant, fearful, in pain, hopeful. And then before too long there was a little baby's loud cry. A baby was born! A baby! It was a little boy with lots of dark curly hair and beautiful eyes searching the face of his mother. Gloria was transported in wonder looking at the little person, counting his fingers and toes, looking at the perfection of this child made in the image of God. Her mother joined her, up for the challenge of grandmotherhood. She hugged her little girl and cradled her little girl's child. The women looked at each other…what was that? It sounded like angels singing and suddenly the room was filled with light. Celestial beings celebrated the birth of this new little incarnation of the Holy. What would the life of this little child be like?

A Peaceable Kingdom with Swans

When Jesus was baptized he knew in a moment the whole of God's realm of Love. When he came up out of that water he experienced, in every fiber of his being, God's unimaginable love and hopeful intention for the world. He hardly had time to contemplate the meaning of this, however, because the Spirit immediately chased him into the wilderness. Jesus was there forty days, tempted by Satan; and he was with the wild beasts; and the angels waited on him. Satan had the usual things with which to tempt Jesus. As St. Ignatius of Loyola would say later, they were roughly described as riches, honor, and pride. But there was an equally powerful temptation and that was to lose the conviction and the hope of that reign of God, the kingdom of Peace that he had glimpsed in that earlier moment.

There were times in the wilderness when Jesus was pretty terrified; he was fully human after all. At other times he could see or feel the presence of the angels and he felt loved and confident. And sometimes, again only for moments, he had sudden glimpses of God's kingdom, the realm of Good, the reign of Peace. While most nights the howling of the wild beasts frightened him, there were other strange times when he saw animals gathered around him. The wolf would be lying down with the lamb. The lion and the deer were curled up together. The jackal rested peacefully upon his lap alongside the rabbit, the eagle sleeping nearby. It was a peaceable kingdom.

At such times Jesus understood that God's kingdom had actually broken into the world. But then the next day the wild beasts would be acting wild and threatening again and he would have to deal with his fear and disappointment. Sometimes he was so disillusioned and lonely and hungry and cold that he was even tempted to lose his conviction that the Realm was a real thing, to believe that he had just imagined all those kingdom experiences, and even tempted to lose hope. But he was Jesus after all, and so instead he came to understand that, yes, the kingdom was breaking into the world, but that it was a verb, a motion, a process. And he understood that he was a part of that action. He realized that the kingdom is here, and it isn't here and we humans are to be partners with God in bringing it fully about.

(Imagined from Mark 1:9–13; Isaiah 11:6-7)

At the end of my thirty-day Ignatian retreat I was out on the rocks at the Eastern Point Retreat House in Gloucester, Massachusetts, standing to watch a beautiful turbulent sea and walking from one large rock formation to another. There was an evening mist in the heat and wind, and I could feel the wetness against my skin. There were other retreatants there too, walking and watching and praying. To me it felt like walking in and out of God. The reign of God is here, it is breaking through, I feel it on my skin, I know it in my heart; and then it is just me, and others, walking on rocks at the ocean, praying that the kingdom will come.

On an earlier occasion during that retreat there was a spectacular full rainbow stretching from the ocean rocks over the little harbor. It was dinnertime and everyone left their seats to rush out to see it fully. Several people mentioned it at the close of the retreat when we spoke with one another, sharing experiences. But I spoke instead of the day that there was a partial rainbow. Because of the fog, perhaps, the rainbow was there but it didn't quite complete itself. It was fragmented. The kingdom is breaking into the world. The lion lays down with the lamb. But it has just begun, and it needs us to embody God's holy loving intention.

The year before the long retreat I had also come to Eastern Point, this time for an eight-day retreat at the end of summer. That summer had been tragic and sad. Youth gangs had formed in many neighborhoods, sometimes organized by crack dealers, sometimes organizing simply to defend their turf from other gangs. A neighborhood had to have a gang. My staff told me of one day when four different gangs hung out on four different corners of the same intersection, all afraid to cross the street because they would be in another gang's territory. And the gangs could be violent, again sometimes reactively—one of theirs was shot and they would try to retaliate. One young boy had been shot on his front steps as gang members tried to shoot one another. Children were dying.

In addition, Graylan and I had decided to separate, and he had just moved out of our condo. I was heartbroken but I didn't know what else to do. How could it be that two people who loved each other just couldn't make it? So, the killing of young people and the personal loss and loneliness all intersected that fall. It was surely hard to see the Good.

And so, when summer ended that sad year of 1992 I went on silent retreat at my beautiful Eastern Point on the rocky coast of Gloucester. I went to pray, to find peace, to find and recapture that "order of God" or "order of the Good" in which to live. I wanted to see the kingdom breaking into the world.

At Eastern Point there is a causeway that stretches out between a small ocean harbor and a small freshwater pond. One can walk along the causeway from the retreat house to a little rocky public beach. Some days if you walk along the causeway at sunset you can see the sun setting on one side and the moon rising on the other. I liked to walk the causeway and sometimes I would sit on a rock and watch the swans on the pond. They were like the swans of the Public Garden pond near my office in Boston, peaceful and entertaining to watch.

One day I noticed that one of the swans had somehow crossed over the causeway and was floating around on the ocean side. It concerned me. Surely swans didn't belong in the ocean. How would it get back to its freshwater pond? I had a deep sense of foreboding and danger for the swan and I wanted to save it, but I felt helpless. I didn't know what to do, but maybe there was somebody to call to help. Maybe there were swan rescuers. I was so tired of unnecessary loss, unnecessary death. I didn't think I could bear to see that beautiful creature lost in a harsh ocean tide.

Two women were coming toward me on the causeway. They were not retreatants, but neighbors out for a walk, so there was no agreement of silence. They saw me watching the swan and smiled so I asked them, "How will the swan get back home?"

One of the women looked at me with interest, and with kindness said, "Oh, don't you know that swans can fly?" No, I didn't know. Thank you. I felt a little silly, but oh, so grateful. The swans I knew in the city didn't fly. The swan had never needed saving, but nevertheless, in my mind, it had just been rescued from certain death and I was so grateful. "Don't you know," said the stranger kindly to the city girl, "don't you know that swans can fly?" And the reign of God is breaking in all around us, all the time.

I hadn't understood. I was simply ignorant. I had walked in and out of God and I hadn't paid attention when I walked out. I forgot about the partially formed rainbow. I forgot to hope. I forgot that the story is not about death, the story is about life. It is about Jesus in the desert with the wild beasts and the lion lying down with the lamb. It is not about losing, it is about finding.

I walked back to the retreat house and suddenly there was a loud whooshing sound. Startled, I turned to see those big wings carrying this beautiful long-necked creature back to its peaceful pond.

Kids don't have to die. It is the desire of Creation that children flourish and grow and live. The kingdom is breaking in and the kingdom isn't here yet. We are part of its creation, called to believe in the good, to hope, to turn around, and repent, ridding the world of guns and drugs, because strangers are kind and swans fly home.

When Jesus finished his fast and recovered, he began his ministry, proclaiming: The time is fulfilled, the kingdom of God has come near – I have seen it. I have been there. Repent, turn around, hope, be part of it; believe in the good news. Believe in the Good. And get busy creating it. (Imagined from Mark 1:14–15)

Massachusetts Correctional Institutions: A Strange Place to Grow Up

Jesus was in the temple one day, teaching a group of us who were gathered around him. Suddenly the scribes and Pharisees came bursting in, dragging a very distressed woman with them. They threw her down in front of Jesus and declared that she had been caught in the very act of adultery. Now she must be stoned to death as the law required. Was Jesus going to follow the law or not? We watched him as he quietly picked up a stick and wrote something in the dirt. Then he looked around to us all and said, "Let the one without sin cast the first stone." Some of us just laughed at that—we knew we were no better than that poor woman, whatever (similar or different) mistakes we had made. We certainly weren't going to be involved in hurting her. The "important" people, though, seemed to change color a bit, looked suddenly down, then backed away and quickly excused themselves. "Is there no one left to condemn you?" Jesus asked. "Neither do I condemn you. Go your way and do not sin again." We were happy and relieved at that and invited the woman to join us as a disciple. Then we went to see what he had been writing in the dirt. (Imagined from John 8:1–11)

The bail was set at $700,000, an extraordinarily high bail for a shooting where the shooter was a youth and no one was critically injured. But the party where the shooting broke out was in Brookline, an affluent suburb of Boston, and the young person accused of the shooting was from Roxbury, a largely African American neighborhood. Hasan, one of our program's peer leaders, was arrested.

It was our custom to appoint two peer leaders in what was then the Damien Funderburg youth program. Hasan showed leadership and good intentions in leaving the street life behind him and moving forward positively with his life. He had recently identified as a Muslim, like his father, and was encouraged in our Unitarian Universalist program to take that seriously. One of the many advantages of being Unitarian

Universalist in a ministry like this is the ability to be inclusive and encouraging of different faith paths.

Like many of the young men who had previously been part of the old Blackhawk gang, Hasan had once carried a gun, but he had gotten rid of it. One day a friend asked him to hold his gun for a weekend when he would be out of town. He did not want to leave it in his room where his mother might find it. Unfortunately, Hasan agreed.

Of course, Hasan did not have to take the gun from his friend, and he didn't have to take it with him when he went out with friends. Perhaps he was afraid that *his* mother would find it—she had been watching him rather closely of late. Hasan went with friends to a party in Brookline; of course, there were alcohol and possibly drugs involved. Suddenly a fight broke out, there was confusion, and there was shooting. Afraid and confused, Hasan drew and fired the gun and hit one of the Brookline youth in the leg. The police arrived during the melee and arrested Hasan. Any other shooters had disappeared.

People of different faith traditions in the neighborhood organized a street vigil to pray for the wounded man's speedy recovery and to pray that things would work out for Hasan. His friends and neighbors knew he was a good person, certainly not violent, and had not been in trouble before. Now he was in a county jail with prohibitively high bail. Hasan's mother and father were both there, Christian and Muslim, separated for some years but united in their concern for their son. Hasan's Muslim father expressed both shock and grief that Hasan could do such a thing, and prayed for the wounded young man who was recovering.

I visited Hasan in the county jail. Because I was clergy, the jail provided a private room in which to visit. I brought Hasan the good wishes of his friends and listened to his many feelings. He was filled with remorse and confusion; he had been high at the time of the shooting and had no clear memory of it. He did not think of himself as someone who would shoot another person and was trying to understand. Since he was there for several months awaiting trial, the jail allowed me to bring him a variety of reading material. His lawyer finally made a deal, and I sat in court and watched as the judge sentenced Hasan to seven-to-ten years in prison. And so, the now eighteen-year-old began his young adult life in prison, for the bad decision made that one weekend to hold and to carry that gun. (And most likely because the shooting happened in a wealthy suburb.) I was reminded of the title of a book by Geoffrey Canada, *Fist Stick Knife Gun*, about the state of urban youth. Without the guns there would have been a brawl perhaps, but less likelihood of serious injury and serious jail time. With adolescents, alcohol, drugs, and guns involved, injury was inevitable. Thank God no one on this occasion had died or been more seriously wounded.

Once Hasan was moved into the state prison system I wondered if I was the right person to continue to visit and support him during his incarceration. Shouldn't this young African American Muslim man have someone more appropriate than a white middle-aged woman visit him, although there was no one else in the Roxbury program able to do so at the time? I mentioned this concern to my son, Lee, and he reminded me of how important his theater director had been to him when he was a teenager. Lee had struggled with all the challenges and temptations of a city high school, and his participation in a citywide youth theater helped him develop his creativity, talent, and self-respect. Lee told me that the director, who was also a middle-aged woman, was an adult who actually really listened to him. She had high expectations of him and fully expected him to meet those expectations; she did not expect him to be someone he was not, but wanted him to develop who he truly was and respect himself. He encouraged me to continue seeing Hasan.

With such encouragement and the hope of providing a genuine presence, I visited Hasan regularly over the next few years. While certainly it is very important to have appropriate role models for young men and women in relation to gender and race, I saw how important it is for people to visit others in jail and in prison, regardless of such categories, and to stick with them. A person in prison can easily lose a sense of self, hope, and belief in possibilities. People on the outside are essential for affirming the basic worth and dignity of a person who is incarcerated, and reminding the person that there is another world out there. And clergy *are* clergy. There is a symbolic significance to that, and we must work hard to be responsible to it, to see the other as a unique and precious image of the Holy and let them know that we see that. We need to continually affirm and embody for them the fact that they are a part of a larger Beloved Community, that their health and well-being is important and that we won't let them go.

Visiting became an important part of my ministry at large, but all visitors are important. Someone who was incarcerated commented to me that prison walls are built to keep people out, not to keep them in. Prisons are often located far away from urban areas, which further keeps the person who is incarcerated alienated from the larger society and less able to adjust after being released. This is in spite of the fact that those who are able to keep in close touch with family and friends are least likely to reoffend.

Hasan was filled with regret for the decisions that he had made and was very introspective, thinking and writing a self-analysis worthy of St. Ignatius himself. He looked at the good forces and bad forces in his life and he genuinely wanted to use his time in prison in some positive way. He wanted to choose life. He wanted to continue his education during those seven years, but there were no educational programs in Massachusetts prisons in the 1990s. On learning this, one of the Urban Ministry's directors, Loretta Ho Sherblom, offered to try to set up a correspondence program for him. She found a willing school and Hasan began the program, but the correctional system kept moving him around from one facility to another, so there was no continuing supervisor to do such things as administer evaluation tests. Eventually, the fact that he was moved around so much made it impossible for him to continue the program.

Nevertheless, Hasan tried to use his time in prison productively. I asked him to design a course for our youth group around issues of violence and its prevention. He developed a very thoughtful course which involved a discussion of street life and its temptations; brainstorming with the young people on the causes of violence; showing the progression of actions and choices which lead to violence. The course included role-plays of several scenarios that Hasan designed, which could lead to violence or not. He suggested acting out the role-play with both a violent and a peaceful resolution, with analysis of what happened in each. The course also included lessons in: the attraction of violence (things that glorify violence, including movies, etc.), substance abuse, and the reality of violence in the community. The Roxbury program staff used the material that Hasan developed and so in a sense, he continued as a peer leader.

Hasan took religion seriously and embraced the Muslim faith more and more. He also had an interest in the Bible and sometimes asked for some direction around understanding it and engaging with it in the imaginative way of Ignatian contemplation. Jesus was a prophet in the Muslim faith and Hasan was interested in learning more about him, as well as using all of the resources he could find in his journey of self-examination and discovery.

Finally, seven years came around and Hasan was paroled. I had just left the UU Urban Ministry and was applying to work at the Pendle Hill Quaker Center in Pennsylvania. Hasan offered to write a letter of reference for me. It was the executive director's favorite reference.

During those years of incarceration Hasan used the time to improve himself, although the corrections department did not make that easy. Coming out of prison he had to face the many obstacles that greet the formerly incarcerated: discrimination in employment and housing, social stigma, lost time, lack of economic resources, a culture of violence and retaliation, and, of course, the internal wounds that result from living in a prison environment. The latter easily fall within a PTSD diagnosis. But Hasan was a bright and compassionate man who wished to live a positive life, and he had family and the support of the Roxbury programs to help him. He has finally been able to pursue his education and become a productive and positive member of the community.

There are more than two million people presently incarcerated in American prisons. Fifty-eight percent of them are African American or Latino. In *The New Jim Crow,* Michelle Alexander suggests that if current incarceration trends continue, one in three African American men will spend time in prison. She argues that the present criminal justice system, with its massive incarceration rate and the many discriminations that follow one's release, constitutes a caste system which continues the historical oppression of black people in America.

There are so many ways that we Americans deprive ourselves of the benefits of creative and productive people in our society. The ease with which guns are purchased and carried takes beautiful lives away from us on a daily basis—both those who are killed and those who suddenly find themselves killers. Our criminal justice system—which is based on punishment, locking people up and away from sight, instead of actually reforming or rehabilitating them—prevents the true restoration of justice and peace to the whole community.

Consider how many of those millions of locked-away people are bright, creative, artistic, thoughtful people like Hasan. Imagine how much they could contribute to our society, if only their gifts were attended to in the criminal justice system. If only this system truly focused on reforming or correcting destructive behavior; developing positive attitudes and skills; returning educated, positive people to the community; and restoring health to the whole community, which is continually wounded by the wounded. The focus of restorative justice is to address the harm that is done when a crime is committed, addressing the needs of the victim, holding the perpetrator of a crime accountable, and seeking to heal the whole community. There are better ways being envisioned to deal with crime than to focus on punishment.

The woman who had been caught in adultery happily agreed to join our little band of disciples to travel with Jesus and learn how to teach and heal and feed others. But first we all went to see what Jesus had been writing in the dirt. It seemed to be a very specific list of sins committed by those pretentious scribes and Pharisees. "Who was without sin?" Jesus had asked, as he made notes in the dirt, detailing those sins. We laughed again, happy to be reminded of God's continuing love and mercy.

Taking Steps

Jesus warned us about easy exorcisms. If we exorcise a few unclean spirits, we'd better be prepared to fill our lives with something else, for example, learning, self-examination, community, friends, and love. Otherwise, we might find our demons multiplied. He told this story: "When the unclean spirit has gone out of a person, it wanders through waterless regions looking for a resting place, but it finds none. Then it says, 'I will return to my house from which I came.' When it comes, it finds it empty, swept, and put in order. Then it goes and brings along seven other spirits more evil than itself, and they enter and live there; and the last state of that person is worse than the first." (Imagined from Matthew 12:43–45)

I looked forward to that glass of wine when I returned home after a long day of ministry. As the executive director, my day was a diverse mix of programs, pastoral care, various crises, and business meetings. I loved that glass of white wine, but let me be honest, it was really two glasses at least and on to two-and-a-half or three.

I was aware of the addictive pattern. After all, I had been part of a church community filled with recovering addicts and walls plastered with sayings such as "An alcoholic alone is in bad company." And I was generally alone after work.

So, aware as I was, I decided on various courses of action at various times. I decided to drink only on weekends, but then the weekends got longer and longer. I decided to drink only wine and beer, but that meant I couldn't have the Manhattan straight up on the special occasions when I went out with friends. Well, the Manhattan straight up and then the wine and then the Drambuie. Maybe two Manhattans, wine, and an aperitif.

Once I had even quit drinking for almost a whole year. But then it was the holidays and why spoil the holidays.

As I said, I was aware of addictive patterns. And it seemed that as often as I would decide to limit my drinking, I would decide to drive home through South Boston and my car would stop of its own accord at the liquor store. What could I do? Just white wine, after all. I rarely got drunk. I didn't think that it interfered with my life. But I knew, deep in my heart, that I was not free and that in regard to alcohol I was full of lies. If I had one drink, after all, I had two. If I had a glass of wine at lunch or at an official event I would always come home and have another one or two later. For the most part, outside of an occasional party at a conference, my drinking was not public.

Finally, I told my longtime Jesuit spiritual director, George Drury, SJ, that I was concerned about my drinking. And the next time I saw George he told me that he had spoken to a recovering alcoholic Jesuit friend about me, and that he would be happy for me to call. And so I met David. Beautiful David, who offered to accompany me to a twelve step meeting.

David was living in a Jesuit house in nearby Jamaica Plain and I met him there. He complimented me in some way on my appearance, in a manner that was friendly and not quite knowing what to say upon meeting, so I complimented him back on his. And he laughed and we went to the meeting. I went to a few different meetings with David and I called him as needed during those first days, but then of course it was time for me to be on my own and probably to have a woman sponsor. David and I would connect over spiritual direction during the next few years as our paths in urban ministry and direction often crossed. Sadly, he died suddenly at the age of sixty. Two great spiritual directors, Jesuits George and David made it possible for me to face my self-destructive behaviors and to find the spiritual freedom that is so central to Ignatian spirituality.

I found a women's twelve-step meeting in a nearby town.

It was a diverse group of women, including high school dropouts and psychotherapists, willing to laugh at some of the dated language in the twelve steps, while honoring and being faithful to the process. They were very serious about sobriety and became a healing support for me for three years. I went on the thirty-day Spiritual Exercises of St. Ignatius retreat after that time, and then only felt an occasional need for a meeting, grateful that it was always there.

I was fortunate to have had what some might call a "high bottom," in the sense that we stop drinking when we hit bottom. I did not suffer the losses of a job or relationships, or home and well-being, that some people suffer. My time at the Church of the United Community helped me to understand addictions early, and I was blessed to have the awareness and help of my spiritual director. I could see the pattern and danger in my drinking, and I had to recognize the continuous internal battle with myself, wanting to move toward health and wholeness, lying to myself about my dependency, making promises to myself that I never seemed to keep. I was familiar enough with twelve-step meetings not to be afraid to attend one, although I did definitely need that friendly presence to go with me to my first (and second!) meeting.

But my own experience underscores the reality that alcoholism and similar addictive patterns are a real danger for people working in high-stress environments where one is regularly confronted with violence. There is the feeling that one can never quite relax, but must be hypervigilant. Mental health practitioners are recognizing that not only is the experience of vicarious trauma common among those who work with victims of violence, but that there is even such a thing as community trauma which can be experienced simply by living in high-crime neighborhoods. Whatever relieves this stress and feels good, and helps one to forget, relax, and to feel safe becomes very appealing. For me it was alcohol and it robbed me for a time of my personal, internal, and spiritual freedom. I am very grateful for the "high bottom." And I am a grateful recovering alcoholic.

One night during my first drinking year, a miserable high school summer, I stood abandoned and distraught and very drunk on my front lawn and literally shook my fist at God looking up to the darkness, and I told God that I no longer believed in "Him." So just go away!

I did not know then that God cried with me for my pain, would fill my life with wonderful others to help me in difficult times, and would *not* go away.

After listening to Jesus's story, we understood that getting rid of unclean spirits is not an easy, one-time exorcism kind of thing. Better to face up, be honest, and deal with one's own demons consciously, with other people and the Higher Power to help, than to pretend they are gone and get a whole host of new ones.

Sacred Lives in Temple and Prison

Anna was a prophet who lived in the temple in Jerusalem. She had lived there for most of her eighty-four years, having been widowed as a young woman. Anna spent her days studying the scriptures, listening to the various scholars and prophets and religious men and women who frequented the temple, and she spent many hours in prayer. Anna was a mystic and visionary and she was convinced that one day she would see something extraordinary there in the temple. Anna believed that she would see a savior, the very presence of God, an incarnation of the Holy. Then one day Anna was filled with joy, for suddenly, as she had dreamed, she saw the face of God. It was not in one of the scholars or the prophets or the religious men and women. Anna saw the face of God in a little baby and then she told the world, "The Messiah is here. God is among us." (Imagined from Luke 2:36–38)

Concord, Massachusetts, is an important historical site. One of the first battles of the American Revolution was fought here and "the rude bridge that arched the flood," as Ralph Waldo Emerson described it, is a popular tourist site. The historic homes of several important figures are open for visiting, including the homes Emerson and Henry David Thoreau. Walden Pond is nearby. Concord is now a woodsy, affluent suburb with strict zoning laws to maintain its pristine appearance. It is also the site of the Massachusetts Correctional Institution at Concord, where in the 1990s all men convicted of felonies were evaluated and then usually sent on to other prisons to do their time.

I had been to MCI Concord several times. This time I was visiting William. Eighteen-year-old William had been a participant in the Roxbury church youth programs for several years but had become involved in the neighborhood drug business. After a shooting incident, he had been convicted of assault with a deadly weapon and was waiting to be classified and sent elsewhere to serve his sentence. He asked if I could bring Tasha, his baby's mother, and his baby, little Willy, out to visit. So I met the young woman and toddler in Dorchester and we began a saga of minor disasters.

Seventeen-year-old Tasha was now pregnant with someone else's child and she did not have much to say as we rode together. I'm sure that she was uncomfortable with me, but she came off as rude and demanding. She grumbled to me that she was hungry, so I stopped at a convenience store and bought her some food. "What about Willy?" I asked. "He's okay," she responded. He wasn't. He saw her food and started crying so we stopped again to get him some toddler-appropriate food.

At the prison I put quarters into the locker for our things. Tasha wanted something from her purse after the locker had closed, so opening and closing it took more of my quarters. The prison does not allow you to bring anything into the prisoner visiting area except for a snack card to prepay for the vending machines, which you can purchase before you go in. Even car keys are forbidden, which makes it mandatory to rent a locker. Sometimes other visitors will make change if you get stuck without quarters, but there is no way to get a locker if you don't have the proper coins. Of course, the prison is located well away from any shops where you might get change.

I don't like any prisons, but I found visiting Concord particularly unpleasant and the staff especially unfriendly. In my experience, they had zero flexibility about even minor rules. I once saw them turn away a young child from seeing his father because the child wore cutoff jeans. The family had driven up from Connecticut for the visit, and the mother could not leave the child alone in the waiting room, so they were both therefore unable to see him.

Tasha had worn sweatpants, common apparel for pregnant girls. The guard told her that they were not acceptable, she would have to wear maternity pants. Tasha grumbled, argued, and swore as I hustled her away before she ended all chance of our visiting. We got our things out of the locker and set out to find her some acceptable pants. Visiting hours were from 6:30 to 8:30 so time was limited.

While Concord boasted many lovely neighborhoods, and a few boutique shops, I was not aware of any big malls or shopping centers open at 6:30 in the evening. I was told where to find a Walmart in a nearby town. It was dark and I didn't know the winding country roads, but somehow we found it and I purchased what must have been the last pair of maternity pants in the store, if not the county. Tasha didn't like them and complained, but agreed to wear them and we hurried back before it was too late to be admitted.

I used my last quarters to get us another locker. When we approached the same guard to enter she looked at little Willy and saw that he had a pierced ear with a stud in it. "You can't wear jewelry. You'll have to take that out." Tasha started swearing; the guard told her to change her attitude or leave. I again hustled her away and we removed the earring as Tasha continued to curse. Since we could not get another locker once ours was opened, I hid the earring on top of the Coke machine. Tasha protested this, but I insisted and we were able finally to get into the visiting area.

William had been waiting for a while and was relieved and grateful to see us, especially his little boy. He bounded toward Willy with big arms open and the toddler, who had not seen his father for a few weeks, was startled and began to howl. Tasha decided to get Willy a soda to calm him down. She handed Willy the soda and we all sat down together but the child was not to be pacified. He took a sip and then threw the can across the room, orange soda flowing everywhere. All the other men and their visitors turned to see what the continuing commotion was about. We had received quite a bit of attention by that time, but finally things quieted down and William reconciled with Willy with hugs and laughter. He truly loved that little child. After the visit, Tasha and I, now more or less friends, retrieved the earring from the top of the Coke machine and drove back to the city.

This young father was a beautiful, intelligent young man. As a younger teen he had impressed our youth program staff with his acting talent and charisma. As a former theater major, I recognized stage presence when I saw it. When William joined in on a production all eyes were on him and the volunteers whispered to each other, "William is really talented!" A career in theater wasn't to be for William, however. He lived in a low-income urban African American community in the 1990s with the crack epidemic in full force, and like many young men he didn't think too much about a future career. Often I heard the young people say that they had little expectation of living much past their teens. They all had friends who had died from violence, and the cycle of shooting and revenge engaged their daily attention, along with the opportunity to make lots of quick money working for the older drug dealers. It wasn't until they were nineteen or twenty that some young people began to think that maybe they would have a life after all, and they had better start thinking about education or training.

This was the world he lived in and talented, charismatic William got into trouble. I never really heard the details of his offense. It had to do with shooting and wounding a drug dealer, something bad in itself of course, but very bad in the long term given that William was young and the dealer an established power in the neighborhood. When William was first arrested I visited him in the downtown county jail. Sitting in the individual visiting booth with glass in between us, William was so obviously a frightened child. There in the county jail, there was no charismatic actor or charming teen, nor was there a street-hardened drug dealer. There was just a terrified kid.

I described my visit to the UU Urban Ministry board of directors at a meeting later that week, and a compassionate and generous director proposed that we bail William out of jail. They voted unanimously to post the $20,000 bond from the agency investments, pending the approval of his family and the opinion of our gang outreach staff. After thoughtful consideration of where William might be better off and whether he could be trusted to appear in court, we posted bail for him and William had a few more months of freedom. The case was settled and he was sentenced to several years in prison.

The visits to the county jail and the MCI Concord were among several that I made to William over the next two years before I moved from Massachusetts. He ended up in a maximum security prison about an hour west of Boston. William was eager to use his time there fruitfully but there were very few educational programs in Massachusetts prisons. At that time I was participating in the Urban Ministry Fellowship Program at Harvard Divinity School and taking a course called Freedom and the Navigation of Desire, which included studying some major thinkers. I decided to adapt some of my homework from the class for William, starting with Immanuel Kant. Kant believed in the human capacity to determine one's life path, to consciously make decisions based on one's most important values determined through reason and experience, rooted in a moral law written on the human heart. Kant said that we should locate and act on maxims, or deeply held principles, that were so significant and central to us that we would will them for everyone. I asked William to identify the core values in his own life that he considered the most important for everyone. Was there anything so important to him that he would completely reorganize his life? We agreed that he would consider this and write to me about it and then we would discuss it.

William loved the assignment and wrote a thoughtful letter saying that his child and his role as parent could motivate him to change his life, and that he believed that caring for those who are helpless and dependent on you, children and others, was a universal value that everyone should follow. From there we considered what changes William would need to make and how he could stick with it through his four or five years of incarceration.

That year I was in the process of leaving the UU Urban Ministry and determining how some of my ongoing obligations could be filled. A volunteer with the Roxbury program had an interest in picking up prison visitation and establishing relationships with the incarcerated young men, and he made a good connection with William.

As it turned out, I accepted a position in another state, but before I left Massachusetts, I visited William for the last time, taking his sister to see him in what was a much less chaotic visit than the earlier one with his child. He had matured during his time in prison, although he undoubtedly experienced some things that are not helpful to healthy development. Nevertheless, he held to the values of caring for family and protecting the weak.

After leaving the Urban Ministry I moved to Pennsylvania to work for Pendle Hill, a Quaker center for study and contemplation, as the director of social witness programs. After living in Pennsylvania for about three years, I received a call from William, still in prison in Massachusetts. He had a friend find my number and arrange a three-way call. He was calling to say that he was getting out soon and that he was looking for a job. Did I have anything available?

I didn't have any open positions, but even if I did I could not imagine that Chester, Pennsylvania, where I was living and working, would be a good environment for William. Chester is a small postindustrial city with a high degree of poverty and violence. It has few of the many resources of Boston.

I didn't hear from William again. One day, I received an online newsletter from the UU Urban Ministry. It included a notice of people connected to the programs who had died that year. And there was William's name. There was nothing about him or about the circumstances of his death, just his name, sadly, among other names. I searched his name online and read a brief newspaper story saying simply that a twenty-five-year-old man had been shot to death in Roxbury. Just another young African American man shot in Roxbury. It didn't say that this was a charismatic child, a loving father, an intelligent and thoughtful young man. Simply that a twenty-five-year-old man had been shot to death in Roxbury.

I was stunned. I still find it hard to believe several years later. William, the vibrant actor who charmed the suburban volunteers. William, a young kid out on $20,000 bail with our whole staff trying to keep him doing constructive things and not give in to the panic and flee. William in the Concord prison, trying to meet and to know his son. William in a maximum-security prison—maximum security! William writing a personal essay based on the thinking of Immanuel Kant. A phone call from William in my new home in Chester. And then there was his name among those lost. It must be wrong. It must be someone with the same name. How could it be William?

Anna in the temple was graced with the experience of seeing God as an infant just born into the world. She proclaimed God's goodness and justice and mercy to all who could hear. All her life she had waited in the sacred space of God's creation, and she received the gift of seeing the face of God in a tiny baby. And I too saw divinity born into the world, this time in a young kid with stage presence; in a frightened child in jail; as a willing dad trying to embrace a crying child. I saw God locked up in a maximum-security prison, trying to figure out how to survive there, trying to discern what to live for and how to do it, and trying to plan his survival back into the world of the violence and retaliation of the street. I saw the light of God in William and I saw what could have been. And what was lost.

Break Day and a Consideration of Sin

There is no question that Jesus was very compassionate. He was known for healing, and forgiving, and feeding, and other life-giving activities. No question about his loving nature. But Jesus could get angry too, and when he was angry, he didn't hold back from expressing it! He was particularly enraged by those who had power and influence over others and used that influence to hurt or to oppress. "Woe to you scribes and Pharisees, hypocrites!" he was known to shout, accusing the religious leaders of preaching pious words while placing unreasonable demands on the poor. "Woe to you rich!" or "Woe to you who are comfortable!" he would cry out, in the face of poverty and suffering. Jesus was especially upset about those who would hurt the most vulnerable, the "little ones." God had created a good and beautiful world, including a diversity of beautiful people, and he hated that which would injure or destroy this good creation. (Imagined from Matthew 23)

I was tired of sin. I'd had enough of it. It was break day and I had just finished the first of the thematic four "weeks" of the Spiritual Exercises of St. Ignatius. During those eight or so days at the beautiful rocky Eastern Point Retreat House in Gloucester, directed by spiritual director, John Kerdiejus, SJ, I had contemplated the glory of Creation and reviewed the history of God in my life. Through meditation and contemplation, I then jumped into the examination of sin, that which destroys the beautiful creation, or as my friend Phillip Bennett says, "that which does violence to love." As directed by John through the Exercises, I had considered sin globally, historically, socially, and symbolically. As he kept reminding me, we were contemplating BIG sin here, not tiny little actions, but the kind of destructive, institutionalized sin that can infuse whole societies—things like racism, sexism, homophobia, institutionalized mistreatment of others, economic inequality, and all that diminishes the sanctity and joy of human life. The question is asked, "How do we participate in that sin?" I had painfully considered how I had internalized and collaborated with sin in my own life, and I sought forgiveness. Finally, I considered God's response to all this alienation and injury—God responds with compassion, forgiveness, and love. Seeing the pain and confusion of her precious human creation, God chooses to be more fully present in human life by sending her child to join humanity and to teach them the way of love.

The first week of the Exercises was completed. After a break, we would launch forward into the second week, learning to know and love the Incarnation/Jesus, and to serve the good creation. A third week deals with the crucifixion, the fourth week with the resurrection, and the Exercises end after thirty days with a contemplation on learning to love as God loves.

OK, Father Ignatius, I understand. I participate in sin. I am a sinner and I am loved. I am a loved sinner who looks forward to the next week of the Exercises, to knowing Jesus more fully and to becoming a disciple, learning how to address sin in the world and to create a community of justice and peace. But now I am just tired of sin.

The retreatants are given a break day at this point in the Exercises to recover and rest. One is not encouraged to go home on break days, but I wanted some things from home. I drove the hour from Cape Ann to Dorchester. Home. I drove through Uphams Corner and after the silence of the retreat I was energized by the music coming from cars, and the colors and activity of the street. I was enjoying this break.

I entered my condo happily, but then quickly sensed that someone had been there. I noticed that there were two books on the table. As I approached, I could see that they were Frantz Fanon's *The Wretched of the Earth* and an Agatha

Christie mystery. Oh yes, surely it was my daughter, Rachel, who was living in nearby Cambridge and was my emergency contact for the condo in my absence. Then I noticed that my front mini blind was broken. I called Rachel at work.

"Rachel, why is my mini blind broken?"

"Oh, uh, Mom, you weren't supposed to be back yet. That's where the bullet hit it. The wall and the window frame have been repaired, but they haven't gotten a new mini blind yet."

The story was that my neighbor, a security guard aspiring to be a Boston cop, had been cleaning his gun next door and the .38 went off. The bullet came through the wall, crossed the living room, hit and broke the window frame, and nicked the mini blind before coming to rest across the room. Another story, heard later, was that the neighbor's younger teen sisters had gotten hold of the gun and were showing it off to some boys when it fired.

My daughter-in law Laura had been visiting earlier that summer and I had taken a picture of her holding my grandson Tucker at just the spot where the bullet had entered the room at full force.

I was tired of sin. I didn't really need this visual aid. But I got the message. I was back in a community that was flooded with guns—a lively, beautiful life-giving community with an economically and racially diverse population, largely people of color, and a community where these terrible weapons were freely available to kids and others to shoot one another. Institutional sin. Big sin.

I returned to the retreat quite finished with the first week, but ready to jump into the second, learning to be a disciple in the journey to bring that ethic of love and nonviolence into the world. There is an exercise at the beginning of the second week, as we move from the consideration of sin into how to counter it in the service of love. Using our imaginations, we are instructed to visualize and personify that force that Ignatius calls the "enemy of our human nature"—that which seeks to call us away from the path of love. I didn't visualize a red demon breathing fire or a cleft-footed goat. I saw an elegant looking man, beautifully, meticulously dressed, passing through Uphams Corner in a subdued but elegant car, just checking on his business. I wasn't sure . . . who was he? Was he a banker, a businessman, a politician, a weapons manufacturer? Or was he checking directly on his business of distributing drugs and guns to poor kids?

Yes, Jesus had a temper. He could not tolerate the abuse or abandonment of any of the "little ones," the vulnerable. Jesus called the people to create a loving community, where the powerful used their power for the good of the whole, not for personal profit, a world where all were safe and protected. When he was arrested, he instructed a supporter, who rose to defend him, to put down his sword, saying, "All who take the sword will perish by the sword." (Matthew 26:52) Weapons served only to destroy and had no place in a beloved community. Who benefited from their creation and why did they exist at all?

You Don't Have to Walk Alone

Jesus was known for doing some rather spectacular things. For example, he was said to have fed large crowds of people with small amounts of food and to have conducted many large healing sessions for a variety of people with different ailments. He was also known to have spoken some very challenging and controversial words. Of course, he never really traveled or acted alone. There were women and men who were always there to engage with him, question him, party with him, relax with him. He would go off by himself often to pray and to restore his spirit, and he would always return to his friends. There were always people there to love him, and for him to love.

Ministers at large in poor and marginalized communities, especially those working directly with violence, experience a certain amount of trauma, along with the community. One can imagine that there is a high level of burnout in such work. How many funerals for young people can one do? People often asked me how I was able to do such ministry for so long, and I can see in reflecting back that there are three essential things that support a ministry of a crisis nature like this one. I must also point out that after twenty-some years I did, in fact, get into trouble and it was to some degree related to a failure to attend carefully to these things. That failure is described in a later chapter, titled "Falling asleep in the garden."

The three things I recommend for support in doing community-based urban ministry are: a spiritual practice grounded in faith; finding and participating in the love and the joy of one's community rather than just the challenges (having fun); and always working with others, never alone. I loved this ministry and the people with whom I was involved, it always felt like a call to me. I felt privileged to be there.

Whether one is Christian or Jewish, Buddhist, or Muslim, or humanist, a regular spiritual practice is important to keep one grounded and sustained. I saw a spiritual director regularly throughout my ministry and did yearly eight-day retreats, as well as the Ignatian long retreat one year on sabbatical. Some people are fortunate in having morning prayer services they can attend; some people meditate regularly. Whatever the form of the practice it is important to attend to it faithfully, and to have some structure in one's life to allow that. I found that the depth of my commitment and the understanding of my calling increased steadily and deeply as I took time and attention to my own faith practice and development.

I have always believed in living in the community in which one ministers. On the one hand we hear the shots fired in the night, but on the other hand, in my case, we can hear and see the annual Caribbean festival marching joyfully down the street. We can eat food from the Caribbean restaurant or the Spanish restaurant or bean cakes from the restaurant set up by the Nation of Islam in response to a violent shooting. I attended an Episcopal church where we marched with a steel drum band on Palm Sunday, walking up a hill singing "Ride on King Jesus." There were community theatre events and stores that sold pictures of Jesus which plugged into electric sockets so that the bright red heart on his chest beat in rhythm. I was evangelized in three languages. I loved my neighbors and watched their children grow. I planted flowers with the children in the spring. I had fun with my neighbors. There was joy in community.

Finally, I found that of critical importance to me in all that I did, was to do things with others, to create and act in community, not to attempt to do anything alone. In the event that one finds oneself ready to launch into doing something new in the community, the first thing to do is to network.

Reach out to lots of others. For an important cause, for work that needs to be done, there are always others to do it with. This not only brings resources and talent to help in the effort, it brings joy, comfort, friendship and laughter.

I have been blessed in the ministry by having a whole host of others to partner with me and sustain me. Looking back through the years, I have so many memories of being helped and inspired by others. For example:

During the first year of the ministry at large:

Thom, Scotty, and I paddled around the pool, swimming at somewhat different levels of ability. (I'm not much of a swimmer, but I try.) That was okay, because we kept stopping to talk, tread water, or hang onto the edge of the pool. We were talking about the nature of the ministry at large. We were at a Unitarian Universalist district conference at the end of the day when the meetings were over. Scotty and I excitedly agreed when Thom said, "We are worker priests!" "Yes, worker priests! That's what we are!" We loved that image as we loved the ministry at large.

Thom Payne was called to develop community programs at the First Church in Roxbury, which had merged into the Ben Frat. Lawyer/minister Scotty McLennan had created the Legal Ministry, seeing to people's pastoral needs while addressing their legal problems. I had been recently called to develop a ministry for women who were victims of abuse. We had different charges, but similar visions, and throughout the years it was one ministry, as we listened to, supported, and brainstormed with one another along with the senior minister, Bud Murdock, who had revived the ministry at large.

We would follow this team approach through the years as ministers changed. Cheng Imm Tan, Peter Thoms, Rubina Qureshi, Peter Coccoluto, Joyce King, George Daly, Sally

Patton joined the teams, along with others from time to time, forming varied, creative, and vital ministries. Cheng Imm organized the Asian Women's Task Force Against Domestic Violence, Joyce oversaw the expansion of Renewal House, Rubina established an after school program in Roxbury and George joined us to supervise Roxbury's developing programs, Peter T. developed the Children's Law Project, Peter C. represented us in various social activist networks, and Sally created a development department focused on our member churches. The work was varied, but always we were there to support one another in our various, challenging ministries. We continued to do our best to be "worker priests."

During the last several years of my Boston ministry:

We sat on kneeling benches and cushions in the Empty Bell retreat center, a statue of Kwan Yin and an icon of Jesus rescuing Adam and Eve from hell gracing the space. Some of us knew each other well, some less well. There was Robert Jonas, the Roman Catholic/Buddhist-inspired spiritual director with whom we were planning to meet regularly. There was my good friend, Scotty, then the University chaplain at Tufts. There was Thomas Mikelson, the minister at First Parish in Cambridge UU, who had organized this experiment, and there was Anita Farber-Robertson, who was serving the UU Church of Greater Lynn, Massachusetts. We had gathered to make a commitment to one another, to meet monthly together with Jonas at the Empty Bell which was then located in Watertown, and additionally once a month for lunch. We were to be spiritual support for one another in our ministries.

Somewhere, somehow, in that first discussion the subject of the Gospel of John came up. There was an immediate, strong, passionate negative reaction on the part of one or two of my colleagues. I gasped internally. "Could I leave?" I thought. "How much had I committed?" I was aware of the problems with John, but it was the gospel that had moved me most, especially in times of crisis. It had seemed to speak to me directly: "I will not leave you orphaned . . . peace I leave with you, my peace I give to you, I do not give to you as the world gives . . . love one another as I have loved you." There were some of my favorite stories in contemplation: the Samaritan woman at the well, the man at the pool of Bethsaida, the woman caught in adultery, Mary Magdalene at the tomb. Could I trust the others to listen to my own spiritual journey when they had such a negative reaction to something that was so important in my own experience?

I could see that Jonas had shared my surprised reaction. With trepidation I spoke up, sharing my feelings. "Okay," the others said. "Let's study and pray with John as our first activity!" It was a generous response and we all relaxed. We met with one another for eight years, once a month with Jonas and once a month for lunch. We called ourselves the Holy Spirit Group, or Holy Spirits. In addition to the spiritual support we offered to one another, we joined together with others to help plan the first Revival!, a gathering of Christian Unitarian Universalists, and to help organize the Tuckerman Coalition, a legislative advocacy group.

My Clinical Pastoral Education supervisor, Rev. Eugene Robinson, gave me the phrase and idea of eternal relationships. We holy spirits are eternal relationships with one another.

(An historical note: in the winter of 2020 Thomas died of the Covid19 virus early in the pandemic. Scotty, Anita, and I met on Zoom with Jonas and Thomas's wife Patricia Sheppard for a remembrance, and following that Scotty, Anita, and I decided to meet regularly again via Zoom. Scotty had recently retired as the Dean of Religious Life at Stanford, and Anita retired from several years of interim ministry. We continue to meet!)

Again, in the early years:

It was late one night when Jesus knocked on my door. Jesus was about thirteen and had been a resident of the Franklin Square Ministry a few months before, along with his mother. Now he stood before me with another young man about the same age. "We've run away from home, Rev, can we stay in the shelter?" I invited them into my apartment. "Okay, tell me what's going on." Jesus claimed that he could not tolerate his mother any longer. She yelled at him and chased him with a broom, and he'd just had it with her screaming. I knew that Ms. Ramos was very emotional and prone to yelling but I had never seen her be physically violent. The other young man had nothing to say but seemed to be enjoying the adventure.

It was ten o'clock at night and I was going to be a speaker at a conference in New York City the next day. I didn't know what to do. I called a friendly social worker with whom I served on a welfare advisory committee. He laid out reporting requirements and suggested that first I separate the boys and talk with each of them to see if I could get a consistent story. Eventually, Jesus said that he would try going home and talking with his mother if I accompanied him. But when we drove up, she came running out of the house with that broom, yelling in Spanish what she intended to do to him (my Spanish was marginal, but I got the gist of it). We went back to my apartment and I made another late night call to my friend, who further advised me. He urged me at that point to call the social services hotline. Emergency workers came to interview the boys and took them to temporary foster care. I actually managed to get a couple of hours of sleep and wake up in time to make my early flight to New York. In my bleary-eyed presentation at the conference, I talked about how, even in the middle of the night, there are those wonderful people willing to respond in difficult times. And of course, I reminded people that Jesus is, among many things, a beautiful and distressed young person of great value, needing our attention, and our collective energy to change the world.

Throughout the ministry:

When Renewal House was born people seemed to come from nowhere to help create and sustain this shelter for women in crisis, including Ann and Rita, Amarette, Gracia, Sally, and Robin Scott Manna who came as a counseling student and followed Amarette as Advocate/Counselor. There were a multitude of talented student interns, volunteers, and community people. When we invited the local youth street gang into the Roxbury church, volunteers appeared in abundance from the community, even our local city councilor, Chuck Turner, volunteered, along with several members of the Narcotics Anonymous community. When there was a need, people came forward to help respond, supporting one another in the process, with time, availability, ideas, concrete support, creativity, and friendship (and sometimes calls in the middle of the night!).

In the institutional life of the ministry, too, people always came forward offering different kinds of expertise and assistance to make such programs possible: service on the board of directors, legal help, fundraising, program development, sharing resources including different professional skills. Nothing is ever really accomplished alone. And in those times when there is not adequate help and friendship and support, it's time to stop and reevaluate what one is doing. I understood in retrospect that when I did not have a solid group of peers with whom I was working in the daily life of the ministry, that I became burned out and acted in a way that was harmful to myself and others, to be described in the later chapter.

Yes, there are stresses and difficult times in community-based ministry, as in all ministries. But the joy of community, the courage of people who struggle against unfair odds but still love and laugh and encourage others, lifts the soul repeatedly. Held in the love of a Higher Power, with others in community, we find the love, the support, the ideas, the inspiration, the solidarity, and the hope to continue joyfully.

Jesus got discouraged too. Sometimes he was profoundly sad, and he wept. At other times he was angry, shouting and calling people hypocrites, turning over the tables of money changers. But other times, when nobody seemed to care or understand, someone would break in at just the right moment. Like when that woman rushed into a dinner gathering and washed his feet with her precious oil and her tears. She touched him. She loved him. She gave him the strength to keep on keeping on, knowing that he was wrapped in God's love and in the love of others. As Jesus' famous apostle Paul would later say, "And now faith, hope, and love abide, these three; and the greatest of these is love." (Imagined from Luke 7:37–38, I Corinthians 13:13)

The Ultimate Housebreak

It was not clear later where Jesus was standing when he gave his most famous speech. Some said it was on the side of a mountain, some said it was on the plain. Nevertheless, people remembered well the words that he spoke and repeated them over and over to one another and to an ever- expanding community.

"Do not store up for yourselves treasures on earth, where moth and rust consume and where thieves break in and steal; but store up for yourselves treasures in heaven, where neither moth nor rust consumes and where thieves do not break in and steal." (Imagined from Matthew 6:19–20)

I could just see the shawl that I had knitted lying somewhere in a dumpster amid various sorts of city debris and garbage. It was one that I had been very careful about, choosing the colors and textures and frequently reevaluating when to make a new colored stripe. The pattern was easy, of course—knitting was my therapy after quitting smoking and it had to be easy to be effective. But that striped shawl pattern, changing colors or textures at will in a simple stockinette stitch, had given me many moments of calm and pleasure. Now the most carefully crafted one had most probably met its end.

This occurred during the second break-in at our condo in Dorchester. The first break-in had happened shortly after we moved in—someone kicked in our back door while we were out, and the alarm went off and they ran. We had the door reinforced. But this time they kicked in the front door and were bolder. With the alarm sounding, the thief ran in, grabbed the VCR and the shawl to wrap it in, and ran off before the alarm company could even notify us at work that day. We reinforced that door. I felt sad about the shawl. It was red and black and brown, with the red dominant, and I liked the way it accented the room. I preferred to think that the thief had given it to a girlfriend, or perhaps to his mother. But it was hardly a professional looking piece, so the dumpster vision was probably not far off.

This second break-in was not the final break-in however, or the most serious one. That was to come later, after Graylan had moved to D.C. and my daughter Rachel, now an adult, had come home for a few months. One night we left the alarm off because our wandering cat, Dandelion, had not come home by the time we went to bed. Without the alarm set, Rachel, who was staying in the downstairs room of the split-level, could simply open her back window to let him in without having to come upstairs twice to turn off, and then on, the alarm. When I came down in the morning Rachel was already awake and told me that yes, Dandelion had come home. But also, she had been up early to discover that a front window was open.

The current VCR was still there, and I didn't see anything else amiss so at first we both thought that someone had tried to get in but was unable to. Then suddenly it dawned on me. I looked to the chair by the front door where my briefcase had been, along with my keys. Empty. I ran to the front door, and onto the porch and yes, my car was missing. My little Acura, my lovely little car that was the first car I ever chose because I liked it, not because it was the cheapest one, my little Integra—it was gone. The number three parking place was empty, and I'm told that I expressed myself clearly and loudly as to what I thought about someone stealing my car. Rachel told me later, "There was Rev. Mom on the front porch, yelling, 'They expletive deleted stole my expletive deleted car!'"

The police came and wanted me to go down to the station with them, which I did. They asked if I would testify in court, and I said yes. But what would I say? I had a car and now I don't? My car was stolen while I was asleep? Then they were finished with me and there I was at the police station in Dudley Square with no ride home. I didn't have change for the bus so I saw a Nation of Islam member selling Muhammad Speaks. I explained my dilemma to him and asked if he could change a ten-dollar bill. He was sympathetic and gave me the change, to which I then accidentally handed him a five. He looked at me with "that look"—the look you give someone who is trying to cheat you, and he didn't believe me when I said it was a mistake. But I found a ten to give him, got the change, and headed home.

Later the police found my stripped car and it was towed to a lot where it was considered totaled. When I drove up to the lot in my rental car I had to take a moment before I could reclaim my belongings from inside what was left of my little Integra, because I began to cry upon seeing it, with its hood ripped off and wheels missing. I collected some Nina Simone tapes and other personal things from inside the car, said goodbye, and went off to buy another car.

In general, I'm not very materialistic. People say that you have a sense of being invaded when there is a break-in at your home. I don't remember feeling that my personal space was invaded. What I felt was rage that they took my "expletive deleted" car. Losing my keys and briefcase was aggravating, too . . . but they took my car! To add insult to injury, the police said that the thief, most likely a young man, probably got a hundred bucks for the car and it was stripped before morning.

I was clearly attached to that "treasure on earth." How easily we become attached to material things. The Spiritual Exercises of St. Ignatius begins by presenting a basic "Principle and Foundation" in which we are advised as faithful people to "make ourselves indifferent to all created things." The word indifferent here means not a lack of concern, but a lack of attachment, so that we can discern daily what is of true value and what is not. Here I am, someone who has done the Exercises and taken Ignatian spirituality very seriously, furious and distressed over the loss of this material "treasure." The whole process of working through the anger and frustration brought me closer to that Ignatian goal of nonattachment, and helped me to focus some of that anger, in solidarity with my neighbors, on the very nature of the experience of living in a high-crime neighborhood. It's not right to take people's things. It's not right that young people climb in your window and steal your car, and that others pay them to do so. It's not right that people can disrespect and trample on your space. All too common experiences in these neighborhoods.

I chose to live in this neighborhood. I believe that ministers should live in their parishioners' neighborhoods and be a part of that larger community, and I love this one. But, during the years that I lived in Uphams Corner there were several alarming incidents much more serious than car theft, including the brutal murder of a young couple in a takeout restaurant across the street from our condo development. Later there was a shooting death behind the development, and on another occasion the windows were shot out of one unit by an angry drug dealer. And this was in a development of working, middle-class people trying to make a good home in the city.

The neighborhood was primarily a community of color—African American, Caribbean, Cape Verdean, Latinx. (Once, walking along Dudley Street, I was evangelized in three languages.) This diversity gave the community an incredible richness of cultures, festivals and foods, and active, colorful street life. There was an old theater with community events, a library, some lovely old houses, and many kinds of shops. It was a good place to live. But why should break-ins, guns, robbery, and drugs be a part of any neighborhood, anywhere? And yet these are problems that are rooted in economic inequality and racism, and therefore they involve us all, diminishing our whole society.

Increasingly, the phenomenon of community trauma, like PTSD, is being recognized by mental health and social service workers, in which people develop forms of traumatic stress reactions simply by living in the neighborhood. Imagine how much courage and strong internal resources people in many communities need simply to live their daily lives.

I certainly experienced some of that traumatic stress. For a while following the third break-in, I would see young men on the street in my community and feel intense anger toward them. "Was it you who took my car?!" I would think. Graylan was very sympathetic about the whole thing and when I told him about my feelings toward young men on the street, he jokingly suggested simply that I run them over.

In the end, it was laughter that helped. The idea of Rev. Ellis cursing loudly on her front porch and fantasizing violent crimes against probably innocent young men. I bought another Integra, grateful that I could, although I was never attached in the same way. I had learned a good lesson about seeking "treasure on earth." I knitted more shawls, hoping that the pretty striped one had found a home and made someone happy. I learned not to put my keys and bag by the door. I thanked God for Rachel's safety and well-being, that Dandelion had come home, and that I was so privileged to live and to minister in God's vibrant kingdom.

"For where your treasure is, there your heart will be also." (Matthew 6:21)

TRANSFORMATIONS

> I know the world is bruised and bleeding, and though it is important not to ignore its pain, it is also critical to refuse to succumb to its malevolence. Like failure, chaos contains information that can lead to knowledge—even wisdom. Like art.
>
> *Toni Morrison*

Falling Asleep in the Garden

Jesus was fully aware of the violence. He had come to Jerusalem with no illusions. Yes, he was intimately close to his Abba/Amma. Yes, he had tasted mountaintop transcendence. But here in the midst of human community there were anger and pride, greed and fear. Here in this bustling city, there was real and immediate danger to him. Jesus would most likely not escape it – it might even be that he would die and die horribly. In great distress, he went to the garden of Gethsemane to pray that it might not be so. We, his friends and disciples accompanied him, and he asked us to keep watch. "Remain here, and keep awake," he said. We were asked to watch, to stay awake, to pray. That's what Jesus, the one we loved so much and followed, wanted us to do. Just stay awake. (Imagined from Matthew 26:36–46)

I was privileged to work for the UU Urban Ministry for twenty-three years, after which I moved to Pennsylvania, where I continued to work in urban ministry in different ways. My departure from UUUM was a painful one. One evening, over dinner with close friends in my new home in Pennsylvania, I was reflecting on the difficult events that led to my departure from the UUUM. "Everybody falls in love," said my Quaker Jungian therapist friend with a bit of surprise in his voice. I had just related to him the circumstances of my leaving my longtime ministry position. I had done so with much explanation as to how I could have "done such a thing." A love affair with an employee, that was bad enough. And someone who on occasion sought my spiritual support, that was worse—but someone presently under indictment for murder?

Everybody falls in love. For a moment after he said that I felt innocent. For a moment, it was simple. For a moment, it was simply about love. And in one sense I guess it was. After all, I was there in the city because of love. For many years and through many changes I had stayed because of love. The Jesuit Pedro Arrupe writes, "There is nothing so easy as to fall in love." But with whom was I in love? Through the years of working in an atmosphere of frequent crisis, I lost my way and forgot who it was I loved. I forgot whose I was.

Our Roxbury gang outreach worker, Jerry, called me from Brigham and Women's Hospital. Erik had been shot, could I come to the emergency room? I went immediately and was taken to a small private room where Erik's mother and Jerry were waiting. The three of us waited and prayed together. After a while the doctor came to find us. The bullet had lodged just to the side of Erik's spine, and they were able to remove it. He showed us the X-ray. Erik would be okay.

Jerry called late one evening. I had just come from the Asian shelter's gala fundraiser. Eddy had been shot, could I come? When I arrived, Eddy's mother, Nancy, had collapsed on the stairs, embraced by several friends and neighbors. Eddy had died in the ambulance and was pronounced dead at the hospital. Nancy was cared for but there were children from the neighborhood outside screaming, crying, and running around in a confused and terrified state. "Eddy, Eddy!" they screamed. Jerry and I gathered them into a circle, and we prayed for Eddy. I asked the children to imagine Eddy in a great light, to imagine the light holding them and to pray that he was happy with God. They were quiet as their parents came to take them home. Through the next days, Jerry and I were a team in handling the media, supporting Nancy, arranging the funeral, and addressing the many reactions of the community.

Jerry called. He told me that he was being indicted on a charge of rape. I went to his office the next day to meet with him and the investigator from the Department of Children and Families (DCF). She questioned him, asking about the physical arrangement of the church, the location of the rooms. She seemed relieved and indicated to me that the young woman's story did not make sense in the context of the space. We hired a lawyer who hired an investigator, and it became more and more clear over the following weeks that the story was not true. The charges were dropped. Jerry came by my office and wept. We prayed.

One day Jerry called me about nothing at all, mentioning that he was with a particular young man named Mike in Mike's car. There seemed to be no purpose to the call, but I knew that there was. He was letting Mike know that he would be named if anything happened to him. I knew that Mike was a troubled and violent young man. Later he would kill and then be killed.

For nine years there were the calls from Jerry. Carl shot and in the hospital. William in jail. Hasan arrested and in jail in Dedham with $700,000 bail. Jason stabbed. Adult gang members at the church.

There were program ideas too, lots of them. Conflict

resolution for the youth, and conflicts around sharing the space with the adults as the programs at the Roxbury church grew. Lots of drama, lots of transformation, loss, gain, sorrow, and joy—always intense. But in the midst of the craziness was a beloved community.

We planned to organize a new congregation at that old historic Roxbury church and things were getting exciting. Jerry was bringing in friends and family to kick off the new church. But that Friday Jerry called: "I've been arrested for murder, please make sure that my son is okay."

I made several calls: to his child's mother, to the lawyer, to the board chair. Jerry was being charged with murder in a shooting that had occurred fifteen years earlier, when he was selling drugs. A young woman had been shot to death on Easter and her family was convinced that Jerry had killed her. They had pushed through the years to reopen the investigation and succeeded. There was much drama. I visited Jerry in jail, and then at the prison where I had visited the others. Bail was posted and Jerry was out to await the trial. It was an emotional and frightening time, and eventually boundaries were crossed. Jerry had been a central part of the ministry in Roxbury, and I had come to consider him a good friend and to depend on him in the most difficult and even dangerous of situations. And in this time of ultimate stress, what was a collegial and supervisory relationship became, for a brief time, something more intimate, and that became confusing and chaotic. It was clearly, as St. Ignatius would say, a "disordered" relationship. Although we were two single adults, there are good reasons for observing appropriate boundaries for clergy and others in helping professions. They provide clarity and safety, order, and appropriate authority. In the intensity of those days, I lost all sense of that. I crossed a boundary that should not have been crossed.

"Stay awake," Jesus said. "Stay here and pray."

I was called and I was in love. For years and years, I was called in love. Not with my friend and co-worker Jerry, with whom I had shared so much. No, not with Jerry. The call was bigger, the love of a different sort. I had fallen asleep and forgotten—forgotten whose I was—and people were hurt. "Everybody falls in love," my Quaker friend said.

Following the disclosure of this relationship there was a time of discernment and negotiation which ended in my resignation from the UUUM. I then spent several months in study and reflection; in part required by the Unitarian Universalist ministerial fellowship committee. I acknowledged the harm that was done through my poor choices and addressed it as best as I could. I also came to recognize the amount of trauma that I had experienced in the previous years, and the effect that it had on my ability to maintain appropriate boundaries. People were hurt, and I was so, so sorry. Deep and difficult lessons were learned. (Jerry was eventually tried and acquitted of all criminal charges.)

During that year of reflection, I was invited to speak at Pendle Hill, a Quaker study center in Pennsylvania. That engagement began a series of conversations, and I was called to a new ministry there. I would develop a program for at-risk youth in the nearby small city of Chester. The work continued.

We disciples tried our hardest to stay awake. We wanted to be faithful. But we were overwhelmed. We were tired and we were afraid and confused and we weren't sure what to do. But we were there because of our love. We were there because God had called us, in love, to be there. When we awoke, we were so sorry, and there was so much work to do, still so much work to do. We would just have to keep trying to do better, to love God and our neighbor, and to try to stay awake.

Resurrection

Early on Sunday morning, Mary Magdalene went to the tomb in the garden where Jesus' broken body had been placed. She discovered that the stone that covered the entrance to the tomb had been rolled away and Jesus' body was missing. She called other disciples, who came to see this empty tomb and then ran back to where they had been staying in fear of the authorities. Mary, however, remained at the tomb and wept, inconsolably. She glanced into the tomb as she cried and suddenly saw two figures appearing to be a man and woman dressed all in white and having a decidedly luminous look to them. They were sitting where Jesus had been laid, one at the head and one at the foot. The sparkling creatures looked at Mary in confusion and asked, "Madam, why are you weeping?" She explained that someone had taken the body of her beloved teacher and friend, and suddenly there was someone with her outside of the tomb. Again, there was the question, "Madam, why are you weeping?" Mary thought that this person was the gardener and she turned to him to solicit his help in finding the missing body, and just then the person said her name. "Mary," he said, and she knew suddenly with her whole being, in the depth of her soul, that it was Jesus. The Resurrection had come. It was all about life. Not death. Not loss. It was about life. (Imagined from John 20:1–16)

After leaving the Urban Ministry, I felt a deep loss and I thought of it symbolically as a kind of Saturday time. The disciples had lost their beloved teacher on Friday, and prior to the resurrection on Sunday, all seemed totally lost. But it was not lost. Love returns and there is work to be done. A new ministry awaited me in Pennsylvania and Saturday came to an end. The journey to Pendle Hill and that new ministry felt like a form of resurrection. It is all about life!

On a hot summer day that August, 2002, my beloved spiritual sister, Rita, came to my Dorchester condo with her two "daughters" to help me pack my car. Rita's parish had helped to rescue the two girls from an abusive situation in

Nicaragua and they now lived in the old convent with her while they finished their education. Rita proclaimed that she had a gift for fitting many things into a limited space and indeed she proved it as she packed up my little Integra. My condo was sold and almost empty, waiting for my neighbor to take the bed that I had slept in that last night for her little daughter. Finally, we put the kitties, Dandelion and Isadora, each in a separate cat carrier, into the back seat. Rita's beautiful Nicaraguan girls wept for Rita. "How sad," one said, "that her friend is leaving." It was a beautiful day and I drove out of my very loved, very known Boston with my spiritual sister waving goodbye. Through vibrant Uphams Corner to the Turnpike, surrounded and filled with God's love and the love of others, on my way to my new ministry adventure. Words of the psalms sang in my head now as they had nurtured me during the last year and would continue to in the future.

> *I shall not die but I shall live, and recount the deeds of the Lord. (Psalm 118:17-18 adapted)*

> *You have turned my mourning into dancing; you have taken off my sackcloth and clothed me with joy, so that my soul may praise you and not be silent. O Lord my God, I will give thanks to you forever. (Psalm 30: 11–12)*

Now in resurrection, I was living in an apartment overlooking a bamboo forest and a small pond with a fountain at the Pendle Hill Quaker Center for Study and Contemplation. Every morning I walked to the main campus past the bamboo, and a magnificent Japanese maple tree, the mother tree for many others. I passed under what I understood to be a Bodhi tree, the kind of tree under which the Buddha achieved enlightenment, through the beautiful grounds of Pendle Hill to the 8:30 worship, worshiping daily in the manner of Friends. The beauty, the worship, the community, and the opportunity to do ministry again were beginning to heal my soul and I knew that I had turned the corner into resurrection.

> *[God] drew me up from the desolate pit, out of the miry bog, and set my feet upon a rock, making my steps secure. God put a new song in my mouth, a song of praise to our God."* (Psalm 40:2–3 adapted)

I was called to a ministry at Pendle Hill to develop a program for youth in the nearby postindustrial and very poor city of Chester. This was to be an outreach program for them, putting the Quaker faith in action. After learning about both communities, Pendle Hill's, and the community of Chester, and discerning needs and abilities, we determined to work with the juvenile probation office. We established an afterschool and dinner program for adjudicated youth with the first goal of keeping them off the streets during the most dangerous hours, and then to provide them with programs to inspire them to change course and to learn means of nonviolence. We hired two local staff people and worked with the community. Pendle Hill resident social action students also worked in the program. After two years of living in the idyllic Pendle Hill apartment, I bought a house in Chester and lived there for ten years before moving to Philadelphia.

The program in Chester and the reality of the difficulties faced by youth there were to cause me more heartache and pain, as the inequality, racism, and injustice of our world took its toll. But the pain and regret of the last year at the Urban Ministry were gradually healing, thanks to the love of others, the wonderful nature of the Quaker faith and its many ministers, continuing prayer and direction in the Ignatian way, and God's spirit of Love which seeks our wholeness and wellness, not our despair. And, surprisingly, among the many things that Pendle Hill gave me was a new relationship, a deep lifelong friendship—Sharon Gunther, whose artistic, generous spirit spoke especially to that part of my soul that needed healing. Joy came creeping back into life.

[God] does not deal with us according to our sins, nor repay us according to our iniquities. For as the heavens are high above the earth, so great is God's steadfast love toward those who fear God; as far as the east is from the west, so far God removes our transgressions from us. (Psalm 103:10–12)

There was ministry to be done. In Chester. In Philadelphia. Through contemplative prayer, I came to feel that I was forgiven by God and that forgiveness is in the very nature of our relationship with God. Forgiveness of others was a matter of time and effort, but not really difficult; forgiving myself remained the spiritual challenge. I understood, however, that too much shame and regret are forms of indulgence in a world where there is so much work to be done. I had spent a lot of energy during the Saturday year facing and accepting my mistakes and my "character defects," so that I was unlikely to make the same mistakes again. Spiritual healing involved giving up the arrogant idea that I was one of the worst sinners in the world, forgiving myself and getting on with it.

I had always and still felt called into ministry, the call from something larger, deeper, more profound that I could ever truly understand. I did not cease to be called because I made a mistake, because I failed a challenge in my life. To be responsible to ministry was to learn, heal, and try to hear God's call and right path in the future, and get on with it. We are all wounded human beings in one way or another. Hopefully our wounds will only make us deeper, better, more compassionate people. That includes ministers, and activists, and all of us who are trying to make a better world.

Mary Magdalene had not always lived an exemplary life. There was a time in her life when she even felt possessed by demons. But then she met a teacher and prophet who seemed somehow to embody all of the truth and beauty and hope and sanctity of life. No matter what she had done or even would do, he loved her with delight and faithfulness. He did not love her naively; when he looked at her she knew that he could see into her very soul and he loved her for this, without condition. The path for Mary would not be smooth following Jesus's resurrection, but she would always be able to touch that place within herself where she understood that she was loved. Not because of anything she had ever done, but just because she was. And that made it all possible. Mary became an important disciple in creating the continuing community of Jesus because there was so much work to be done.

Can Anything Good Come Out of Nazareth?

Philip was hanging out with John the Baptizer when he met Jesus. He was excited as he watched a dove descend on Jesus, and as he listened to his words. Could this be the promised messiah? At the very least he was a prophet! Philip hurried to Nathanael to tell him about it. Nathanael was skeptical, however, on hearing that this Jesus came from a small, insignificant village in Galilee. "Can anything good come out of Nazareth?" he asked. (Imagined from John 1:43–46)

Chester is a small post-industrial city on the Delaware River. The oldest city in Pennsylvania, it was founded and named by William Penn, who first landed there on his trip up the river. Once a vibrant city, Chester's shipyard employed thousands of people, and other manufacturing and supporting businesses employed many more. In the first half of the twentieth century, Chester was part of a migration of southern African American workers seeking a better life and finding it there. The little city became a vital and lively place. People came to shop in Chester from the surrounding communities, and there was a vibrant music scene, spawning stars like Ethel Waters and Bill Haley and the Comets. Martin Luther King Jr. attended Crozer Theological Seminary in Chester and did an internship in a Chester church. It was a place where you could work hard and achieve a prosperous middle-class life. And then, in the1960s, the shipyard closed, sending all those jobs overseas. Other businesses rapidly moved or closed. People with work skills moved to other communities for other jobs. Those with fewer skills and little choice stayed. Chester was once featured on national television as the poorest small postindustrial city in the country. Subsequent efforts to bolster the economy of Chester—a state prison, a wastewater treatment plant, a casino—did little to improve the health or self-image of the community. Environmental justice became an ongoing issue for Chester residents. A soccer stadium was added later and built in such a way that one could approach it directly from the highway without ever having to go into Chester.

I first learned about Chester while in the process of applying for the position at Pendle Hill. Pendle Hill planned to establish an outreach program there, and so as part of the process of considering this ministry I rented a car to explore this little city. I set out at first to find the river.

Before leaving Boston to visit and consider the position, I had looked at Chester on a map and was happy to see that it was on the Delaware River. I had always lived near a body of water and considered this an important part of my life. "As long as there is a way to be at the water, to walk, to sit, to look, to contemplate, I'm happy," I thought. "I understand that Chester is very poor, but it has a river to restore one's spirit!"

Now, however, I was driving around Chester looking for the river. Every road I took in the right direction ended with a dead end, or a large, closed gate and an institutional-looking set of large unattractive, usually abandoned, buildings. The river was apparently behind them, but I couldn't find a place even to see it! My search also took me through neighborhoods where it looked like a bomb had gone off.

After continuing this pilgrimage, I finally discovered a promising route. Winding my way through neighborhoods and over railroad tracks, I found myself under a large bridge at a small asphalt park and boat landing. There was the Delaware River, wide and full-flowing beneath the high bridge. There were a couple of men fishing and a few people there to just watch the river flow and feel its breezes.

I saw a woman there with a child, her grandchild it turned out, and approaching her, I introduced myself. I said that I was considering moving to Chester to work for a faith-based program nearby. What could she tell me about Chester? "It's not as bad as they say," she replied. "It's not as bad as they say" —her first words to describe her home.

Later, after we had established a program for adjudicated youth in Chester, some of the young people said much the same thing when asked to describe their city in a poetry writing workshop led by one of the Pendle Hill students. The youth frequently expressed the feeling that simply living in Chester gave a person a bad name. They had a tragic sense of awareness of violence and young death, as well as an expectation of incarceration, which would be considered extraordinary in a more affluent community.

James was an appealing young man with a particularly difficult childhood. His older brother had been in the program earlier, and his younger brother would follow. He was intelligent and cooperative, but his profoundly sad eyes carried the weight of the pain he had experienced in his brief seventeen years. He had been with his father one evening in Chester when his father was stabbed in an altercation. James managed to get his bleeding father into the car, and not knowing what else to do, he drove to his house, even though at thirteen he had barely driven a car. He ran in to get his mother, but when they rushed out to the car and opened the passenger door his father fell out and died there in front of his home.

James carried the sorrow of that moment into the following years of street life and drugs, but when he was referred to our program by the probation officers he seemed to want to change. He willingly participated in the program events: anti-violence workshops; dinners at Pendle Hill; art, writing, and photography workshops; and a visit to Sharon's photography studio in the city for a photo shoot. James was excited about meeting Nobel Peace Prize laureate Mairead

Corrigan Maguire, who made a special trip to Chester to talk with our young people and others after giving a speech at Pendle Hill. James held back shyly and maintained the appropriate Chester gangster pose until greeted by Maguire, and then that gentle sweetness showed itself in a big smile, as it so often did.

Pendle Hill began to have one or two of the young people work on the grounds and in the kitchen, to be paid and to gain experience in the world of employment. I left it to the Chester program staff to pick the first two candidates. When I next saw James at the program he was withdrawn and disgruntled. "Who wants to work for a few dollars an hour?" he grumbled. I assumed that he had wanted the position, but had not been chosen. While I trusted the judgment of the staff, I was disappointed that he wasn't hired. James's sensitivity and his sorrow continued to move me and I liked him very much. I had hope for him.

James finished the program and his probation and he moved out of my life as did so many beautiful people that I have been privileged to know, if only for a short time. One day, after I had retired from Pendle Hill, my former staff person called to give me devastating news. James had been killed. He was walking away from a fight and was shot in the back. Later, his older brother Mark would also be shot to death in a continuing cycle of violence and retaliation that sometimes went back generations. When we asked the young people in our program to list their hopes and dreams, the first hope that one of them listed was that "nobody in my class gets killed or locked down." Not your typical high school dreams for middle-class white America, but too typical for cities and low income African American neighborhoods like this one. These were bright, creative young people, some of whom went on to college or vocational training, using whatever was offered to them to get out of the lifestyle that had led them to be on probation in the first place. But they faced significant obstacles.

Chester has many beautiful, dedicated people and there are many good things to say about this little city. I lived there for ten years, and I know that there are nice neighborhoods, a beautiful park, a university, a newly developed trail by the river, and some wonderful, dedicated people. But after hearing the news about James, I thought, "Yes, in some ways, Chester is as bad as they say."

Can anything good come out of Nazareth? Can anything good come out of Chester? Nathaniel looked at Jesus and all he could see was a poor peasant from a little uninteresting village. Nobody who is anybody comes from places like that, he thought. But then he looked again and saw that spark of divinity in Jesus, he looked and saw, as Quakers would say, "that of God." Nathaniel stopped and listened and saw the messiah. And I stopped and looked in Chester. I too saw divinity; I saw that of God. I saw a beautiful, wounded young man named James with great potential. He was God's precious, beloved child. And yes, he came from Chester.

Eddie: A Free Man

Traveling with Jesus was getting very stressful and scary. He had challenged the establishment, and they were trying to trip him up, to embarrass him, to discredit him, to disrupt the power he seemed to have within the community. He was attracting more and more followers there in Jerusalem, and lately he was critiquing the Pharisees, Sadducees, and lawyers more and more. This could get dangerous. Jesus, however, was clear about his mission. Rooted in his deep faith, he continued to speak with great power and clarity. For example, when asked which was the greatest of the religious commandments, he answered, "You shall love the Lord your God with all your heart, and with all your soul, and with all your mind. This is the greatest and first commandment. And a second is like it: 'You shall love your neighbor as yourself.' On these two commandments hang all the law and the prophets." (Imagined from Matthew 22:34–40)

The Graterford State Correctional Institution looks exactly as you would imagine a prison looking. Although the Department of Corrections is currently in the process of building a new facility, the old structure is a huge grey weather-beaten stone fortress with guard towers on all corners and coils of barbed wire everywhere. I am very familiar with the process of visiting here, having done so for several years. Sometimes when you drive up to the prison they will be checking cars, and you are pulled over to wait while two guards and a dog search your car. Finding no drugs, they let you continue. Inside, you are processed, you get your vendor card for snacks and your locker (if you have the $10 deposit), and wait to be called to be screened.

Occasionally there is a problem. One day during a heat wave, the processing guard considered my blouse too low-cut. I was astonished and embarrassed, a seventy-year-old minister, never having considered this particular blouse in the least daring. Two other guards seemed to agree with me when

I asked them for directions to the nearest clothing store and explained why, but that didn't change things. I got directions, drove to the Dress Barn in a nearby town, and returned wearing a new blouse for the visit. You can never tell with prisons. I once visited a person in a county jail in New Jersey, also in the summer, and they wouldn't admit me with sandals on. I had to buy a cheap pair of plastic shoes at a nearby Dollar Store. But sandals are okay at Graterford. Now I always wear a clergy shirt and shoes, heat wave or not!

I visit Graterford to see Eddie, for whom I have been the spiritual director for more than ten years. He completed the full Spiritual Exercises of St. Ignatius and is currently revisiting them in an adaptation based on the theology/cosmology of Teilhard de Chardin.

I met Eddie while on the staff at Pendle Hill and went to Graterford prison for a weekend advanced training program called Alternatives to Violence (AVP). This program operates on an inside/outside basis; Eddie was the facilitator from inside the prison along with a leader from the outside. AVP consists of experiential workshops on conflict resolution and transformation and teaches participants to be group facilitators. As Eddie explained to the group, AVP had helped him to identify and deal with his triggers and reinforced his self-esteem. He emphasized that it was based on a belief in the inherent dignity and worth of every person, teaching participants to be open to new and creative ways of finding nonviolent resolutions to conflict.

Eddie is serving a sentence of life without parole (LWOP), otherwise known as "death by incarceration" or, as Pope Francis calls it, the "hidden death sentence." When he was twenty-one years old, an addict high on drugs and seeking money to buy more drugs, Eddie killed the owner of a restaurant during a robbery. His memory of that night is vague, as he later described to me:

"I don't remember a lot of details of that night, but I do recall hearing the word come over the loudspeaker from the back of the paddy wagon that the proprietor had died. I remember at that moment feeling totally alienated from the world I once knew; the full magnitude of what I had done came crashing down upon my shoulders. When the PCP laced with cocaine and the liquor wore off, I woke up in a holding pen with thirty to forty others who had also been arrested in the night. The smell of stale urine and last week's garbage hovered like a cloud over the atmosphere. Any hope of this being a terrible nightmare at that point was out the window. All I could see was a long dark tunnel ahead."

A few weeks after he was arrested Eddie had what he calls a spiritual awakening. A visiting minister had preached a sermon on God's love and forgiveness, saying that God's love was unconditional and that God could forgive us even those things we cannot forgive ourselves. Eddie said that he prayed, "LORD I seek your forgiveness today for the wrong I've done. I receive and thank you for your forgiveness, but there is one other thing that I need, LORD, which might be more difficult…I need you LORD to help me forgive myself for what I've done. That part seems impossible to me right now."

Eddie wished to be accountable for what he had done and, as he said, threw himself on the mercy of the court, pleading guilty and waiving a jury trial. He did not understand when he accepted the sentence of life that it was without the possibility of parole. Pennsylvania is among only six states in which a life sentence does not allow parole under any circumstance. It was not until he began serving time at Graterford that he realized what a life sentence meant. It had not been explained by either the attorney or the judge.

During the more than thirty years of his incarceration at Graterford, Eddie has pursued self-examination, education, and spiritual and moral growth. In recent years, he has been deeply involved in the Restorative Justice (RJ) movement. RJ places an emphasis on our interconnectedness and shared humanity. With a focus on the crime victim, RJ emphasizes personal accountability and recognition by the offender of the harm that has been done. With that awareness grows a desire to give back. The program aims to restore health and well-being to the whole community that is wounded, rather than to emphasize punishment. For Eddie, this has meant doing everything he can to help others. He said, "I learned that a huge part of my journey toward healing, redemption, atonement, and transformation would involve giving as much as it would be learning how to receive."

During the AVP weekend, Eddie and I talked about faith and when he learned that I was a spiritual director in the Ignatian tradition he asked to know more. After exchanging a couple of letters I visited him, and we agreed that I would direct him through the Exercises. Eddie has been a Christian throughout his time of incarceration and has worshipped and studied in a variety of ways. He is conversant with liberation theology. He dove into the Exercises with enthusiasm and creativity.

It took us about a year and a half to do the entire Exercises, with monthly visits and exchanges of letters in between. After that, I continued to visit as his spiritual director. In the style of Ignatian direction, I listen to his spiritual challenges and discoveries, give feedback, and make suggestions for his prayer and study.

Eddie is very active in the prison. In addition to his leadership in both AVP and Restorative Justice, he recently completed his BA in a program run by Villanova University.

For the last few years he has also been a hospice worker within the prison and has sat vigil with a number of men during their last minutes and hours. He is readily available to listen and encourage his peers, staff, correctional officers, or anyone else with a need or a burden.

Eddie faces the same challenges as any minister or activist. Often he does too much, gives too much of his time, and ends up over-scheduled and exhausted. He also experiences the joy that any minister or activist knows when he sees people learn, and their lives change and benefit. He is very serious about his faith and this, too, gives him joy, as he has deep moments of knowing the presence of the Holy (whom he most often calls "She!). He is part of a vibrant prayer group which meets regularly and has particular times in the day when the men pray for one another, no matter where they happen to be at the time. His institutional job is as a peer assistant for the Substance Youth Disorders Department. He leads certain self-help groups and has co-led, with a therapist, a "co-occurring" group for men with both addiction and mental health issues. Of course, he does all this while living in the dreary, hot, fortress of prison, with all the particular limits, dangers, and stresses of that environment.

It goes without saying, Eddie is the kind of person that the leadership of a correctional institution would want to reward for his effort. On the contrary, one recent night, guards came to Eddie's cell, told him to come out, handcuffed him, and demanded that he go with them. Seven guards accompanied him, refusing any explanation, to a restricted unit in the prison. When he asked what he had done he received no response. Then he was put in a cell where he was locked up for twenty-three hours a day. It was almost twenty-four hours before he found out why he was there. He was being accused of having an inappropriate relationship with the therapist he assisted in the co-occurring group. This was completely shocking and bewildering to him.

At first Eddie had no access to a phone or any of his addresses and phone numbers, so he was unable to communicate with anyone on the outside. He received none of his mail. The chaplain brought him a Bible and other reading material (including St. Augustine's Confessions), as well as the love and good wishes of the other men with whom he worked in so many activities. Eddie spent his twenty-three hours a day reading, journaling, and praying. He read and prayed all of the Psalms. He was also able to get his hands on more reading material, including Nelson Mandela's Long Walk to Freedom.

Eventually, Eddie was able to communicate with others on the outside and one of his supporters got him an attorney. I was out of the country for most of this time but received a call from him when I returned. I was shocked at the unexpected and bewildering news, and I could hear the trauma in Eddie's voice. Taken away in the night, put in isolation with no explanation and no knowledge of any process for getting out. He was basically in a prison within the prison with absolutely no power or control over his circumstances. His good behavior over the previous thirty years meant nothing.

During that time, Eddie wrote in a letter to me:

"I found out yesterday that the administration's investigation has been completed and they are going to transfer me. They are actually saying in their report that I am a threat to this facility. This whole situation has been surreal (very difficult at times to believe). I continue to pray for those who are behind this and look to God for the ability to respond always with love. "

I planned to visit Eddie in the restricted unit, but then, abruptly, he was sent back to his regular housing unit with very little explanation, simply that there had been a mistake. He had been in the restricted unit for just over forty days, a time with appropriate religious significance for him (like Moses, and then Jesus in the wilderness). Over time, he learned that a visiting staff member from another institution had briefly sat in on the co-occurring group and felt that Eddie was leading the group rather than the staff counselor. She reported that the group seemed to be Eddie's group rather than the therapist's. This somehow, with a lot of twists and turns, became an "inappropriate relationship."

Restricted unit? Shackled, taken away in the night? Twenty-three hours a day in a cell? As Eddie said in one of his letters to me, he had been at Graterford for more than thirty years, had never been in a fight, never cursed at anyone, never done anything but try to help others and improve himself and to live a life of service.

He insisted that there was never an inappropriate relationship, and the therapist continued to work at the prison. Certainly, if there had been any truth to the accusation, she would not have been able to remain. I had to wonder about the real reason for isolating Eddie. Was it an issue of power? A way to keep people who are incarcerated from asserting leadership in a context where keeping them "in and under control" is foundational to the underlying philosophy of our "correctional" system? Of course, there are physically dangerous and threatening people, but Eddie isn't one of them, as everyone knew. He had been there for decades without creating a problem. Was he perceived as dangerous in some other way? Was it threatening to have an incarcerated, African American man be the true leader of a group of recovering people within the prison? Was Eddie just having too much influence? Many of the staff and correctional officers privately expressed their confusion and regret to him for what had happened.

While in the restricted unit, Eddie said in a letter to me:

"Elizabeth, I see so much human and often divine potential in here (too often too many of us inside don't see it). The administration has no problem seeing and relating to us on the inside as "inmates" but some have a problem with seeing us as evolving human beings. I talk, think, and (with my many limitations from being incarcerated) live like a free man. Some people envy that . . . that a person could be in prison for as long as I have and still experience a certain measure of freedom that many do not have/have not experienced on the outside."

The experience was truly a traumatic one and will take time to heal. Eddie experienced some benefits, however. Like many of us in ministry, Eddie overcommits himself to good causes and to helping others and becomes spiritually and physically exhausted. The restricted unit gave him time to pray and to read and to journal. In some ways, he felt revived. Reading Mandela and others renewed his interest in liberation theology, and he had a desire to pursue an Ignatian spiritual path more seriously, remembering its emphasis on love expressed in daily actions. "Love ought to manifest itself more by deeds than by words" - St. Ignatius of Loyola. It is the life of the contemplative activist—or active contemplative, as Jesuits say. Eddie resolved to try better to reserve time for himself for prayer and study along with his work in love.

As a symbol of renewed life and intention, Eddie decided to cut his hair after he returned to his regular housing unit. This was not a minor event in his life. Eddie had decided not to cut his hair thirty years before. In accordance with scripture in the Hebrew Testament (Numbers 6:1-6) directing a "Nazirite" to grow his hair as a symbol of his sole dedication to God, Eddie decided that he was too self-absorbed and needed to put God first. Letting his hair grow would be a daily reminder. Now, thirty years later, he had impressive dreadlocks. He asked a friend whom he holds in high esteem, and who also has dreadlocks, if he would cut them, knowing that the friend would understand the significance of those many years and many locks. First, he would understand the thirty-plus years of struggle involved in growing and maintaining the locks; and second, he would recognize Eddie's desire to embark on a new life. They approached the task as a sacred ritual of transformation.

Like a baptism, in which one dies to the old life and is reborn, Eddie was ready to commit himself, a free man, to new life. In an essay on why he was engaging in the Spiritual Exercises again, Eddie wrote:

> It is not enough, Lord, for me to save my own soul if it's at the expense of others never discovering who they are or having the opportunity to join with me in the process of becoming your hand, legs, eyes, arms, mouth, ears . . . your presence here. Prepare me, Lord, for such an undertaking. Help me to help myself by helping others and always speaking up for the voiceless. Help me, Lord, to be there for those who feel they've been counted out.
>
> Let me be a voice for the disempowered, our animal friends, the environment, and most certainly my neighbor. Help me, Lord. Grant me the courage to speak truth to the powers that be. Help me, Lord, to be conscious of the POWER that originates, exists, and flows only from you. Lord, guide me in the process of fulfilling my purpose.

Eddie resumed his important work within the facility and took a step he had been intending to take for some time—he requested papers to begin the process of applying for commutation of his sentence. Those with the "death by incarceration" sentence have few options. Some well-intended activists who have worked hard to end the death penalty and offer LWOP as an alternative are unaware of the harmful effects of life without parole for individuals and for society: there are alarming racial and economic disparities in sentencing; it's incredibly expensive; the state does not guarantee lawyers for appeals, as it does in capital cases; it's vulnerable to bad lawyering; once sentenced, offenders are forgotten. Offenders are often very young when committing a crime, and while the Supreme Court has recently ruled that juveniles cannot receive a LWOP sentence, those eighteen years and older can. The difference of a few days in age can have lifelong consequences, and the whole community suffers.

Eddie is clearly a minister on the inside of the prison. He has positively influenced many lives and continues to do so. Certainly it is time, if there is any sense of justice in the criminal legal justice system, for Eddie to continue his ministry with the rest of us.

A 2021 Addition: The old Graterford prison has been closed and a new, modern prison, Phoenix, has opened next to it and Eddie has moved into the new prison. There are some improvements, such as air conditioning, that are a help for those who are incarcerated there, but while lifers often had their cells to themselves in the old prison, now they must share them. A cell is quite small, most of them are 12′ by 6′.

During the Covid 19 pandemic in 2020-2021, Eddie got a new cellmate, we'll call him Robert. While Eddie is in his fifties and African American, Robert was a white man of about thirty, and a conservative Trump supporter. Eddie is very progressive politically and religiously. Because of the pandemic, they were locked in their cell together for all but about 15 to 40 minutes a day. It was during the 2020 election and the political environment of the whole country was very tense. The two men had many conversations.

Both were Christian and while they may have differed theologically, they shared the same language and symbols, and they used that as a connecting point. They agreed that they were both created and loved by God and worthy of respect, and when things got too tense in their conversation, they would remind each other of that. In addition to politics, they talked about such things as the Black Lives Matter movement and white supremacy—these were some of the tensest conversations, but always they would come back to the mutual respect.

Robert was eventually paroled and after he had gone, Eddie found a letter that Robert had left for him. In it Robert spoke of the profound learning that he had experienced, thanks to Eddie. His views had significantly changed, and he thanked Eddie for respecting him, saying that Eddie treated him so much better than his friends on the outside did. He expressed his deep gratitude and said that Eddie was family to him, and he would be grateful forever.

Eddie, in his wisdom and kindness, continues to transform the world.

Jesus envisioned a world in which we belong to one another in love and responsibility. He called it the realm or reign of God, or the kingdom of God, and asked us to pray that it be on earth as it was in heaven. Teaching us that the spirit of that realm exists among us and within us, Jesus charged us with living it, with co-creating with the Holy a society of love on earth. It's a very difficult task, of course. In the middle of all that human emotion and experience – the wounds, the anger, the fear, the greed – Jesus challenges us to love one another and to continuously forgive. He gives us love as a kind of constitution: Love the Holy Creator/Mystery with heart, soul, and mind, and love one another. On these two commandments all action and choice must be determined. Love the Holy. Love your neighbor.

Michael, Like the Angel

Let mutual love continue. Do not neglect to show hospitality to strangers, for by doing that some have entertained angels without knowing it. (Hebrews 13:1–2)

The people were anticipating the arrival of the kingdom of God. Surely there would be all manner of celestial beings involved, and of course there would be trumpets and strings and great musical sounds to announce its coming! Of course, it would be preceded by a few earthquakes and floods, and then magnificent horsemen would ride in on great steeds, and finally will come the Messiah, the greatest of all great kings. Then there will be a world of peace, freedom, justice. And so God's kingdom will come! The people had some exciting and dramatic ideas! (Imagined from Luke 17:21)

I don't know how long it has been since I have witnessed such pain.

As a volunteer at the weekly food pantry at the Philadelphia Episcopal Cathedral, I checked people in and came to know many of them, offering pastoral support on occasion, enjoying the community. At noon I participated in a liturgy, joining the priest to offer healing prayer to those who so desired.

A young, slight, African American man asked to speak with me. I asked how I could help. At first, he said that he needed to confess, and then that he wanted an exorcism. I told him that I was a minister and that I would pray with him. We went to a quiet corner.

First, I listened. He did not want to hurt anybody, he said. "I don't want to hurt any women," he told me. He did not want to hurt anybody, he kept repeating, but he was angry. "So angry!" he said. It spilled out of him.

I listened and then I prayed with him. He said that his name was Michael. "Like the angel," he said, with a little, sad, laugh. He cried when I prayed for him. He said he didn't like to cry in front of others. He didn't want people to know what he felt. I told him that I was like that too, and that it says in the Bible that God holds every tear we shed, that's how much God loves us.

He continued in agony to say that he didn't want to hurt anyone. "But the voices. The voices." I suggested that he needed mental health help. He said he didn't want to take pills anymore.

"Oh, I am so sorry, Michael." Of course he didn't want to take pills. I understand that. And he was in such pain. "But God can be in the pills, Michael. God doesn't want you to suffer this pain."

"Tomorrow is my birthday. I don't want to be in the hospital on my birthday," he said. When I first said that we would pray he gave me his hand. I wouldn't have initiated a touch, he was so upset and fragile. But he wanted to hold my hand and he squeezed my hand when I prayed.

The liturgy was starting and I was to participate in the healing prayer part of the service. I wanted to let the building manager, know the situation but I didn't see him. I asked Michael if he would sit quietly and he said that he would, and he did. I stood where I could see him, sitting quietly. I was aware of several able-bodied men among those waiting for the food pantry to open, men who I thought could handle things if Michael lost control. He told me that he had no weapons.

In the Gospel message that day, Jesus spoke of the kingdom of God, the reign or realm of God; what the world would be if love was the foundation, if it was the law of the world; a time of peace and equity and healing and justice.

Cathedral Dean Judith Sullivan and I did healing prayers with those gathered around the table.

After the liturgy, after the bread and the wine, I went back to Michael. He was quiet but when he started to talk it was clear that he was still tormented, anguished, and wrestling with his demons. "I don't want to hurt anyone," he kept saying, but there was a rage that felt like possession to him. I went to find the building manager, who said that he had heard Michael talking about violence and that he had already called the police.

They came, at least five of them. Black and white. They talked with Michael and explained to me that they could not take him anywhere unless he said one of the "magic words" indicating violence to self or others. They continued talking with him and finally Michael requested that he be taken to a specific mental health facility, one that he knew well. The officers told us that they were taking him there and they all left together.

Michael told me that he was afraid of police, that he had once been tasered. It is all in the news, of course, black men abused by police. And there was Michael (like the angel) surrounded by big burly guys with guns. There was little Michael, terrified. The officers were professional and treated him kindly. But I hope that he did not feel betrayed. I had asked him to sit quietly, and then the police arrived.

Who knows, perhaps we actually entertained an angel that day, a wounded angel. A stranger walked into the church and he needed help. He felt possessed by demons and he wanted an exorcism. I couldn't get rid of the demons, but I taught Michael the Jesus prayer to use against them. "Lord Jesus Christ, son of God, have mercy on me," a mantra to be repeated. Maybe it will help. I assured him that the demons had no power in the face of Jesus, in the face of Love.

Michael, like the angel, came looking for help and we did what we could. We couldn't let him hurt others as the voices were telling him to do. Michael didn't want to be in the hospital on his birthday, but more than that he didn't want to hurt anyone. His basic goodness, or perhaps it was his angel, was in a wrestling match with his demons. He wanted an exorcism; he will get medication. I hope it helps him.

And I wonder, what about that kingdom of God? How do we create a better world? Where Michael would be loved into health. Where his angel spirit would defeat those demons. Is that possible? Could we dedicate numbers of people to such a troubled one to just stay with him and love him? What good work that would be for the right people—simply to be with others, to love them.

After it was all over, Lilly, one of the food recipients, asked me if I was all right. "You're so kind," she said. "I know you take these things hard." Our angel was taken away in a police car and Lilly wanted to be sure that *I* was all right! "Jesus Christ, child of God, have mercy on us."

Jesus listened to the people's dramatic vision of the kingdom of God's arrival with some amusement and some distress. "No, no, no," he said. "The kingdom of God is not coming with things that can be observed…for in fact, the kingdom of God is among you." He explained that we are the co-creators with the Holy to bring it into full being! We must be a part of creating this world of peace, freedom, and justice! (Imagined from Luke 17:21)

Using Your Gifts

If you bring forth what is within you, what you bring forth will save you." (Jesus, Gospel of Thomas #70)

In this book I tell the stories of many beautiful and brave people, people who faced painful and difficult circumstances in their lives due to unjust or disordered social circumstance: I have told stories of domestic violence and gun violence, addiction to drugs and alcohol, a prison system that represents a new form of racial oppression as well as being cruel and ineffective. These stories go back twenty, even forty years, and sadly the conditions that created them have only gotten worse. Recently, as I revise this manuscript, we have been experiencing an historic pandemic for which we were totally unprepared, and resulting in record numbers of domestic violence incidents, increased drug addiction, and gun violence, with homicide rates breaking all records. Those who are incarcerated have been forced into lock down, confined to small cells, for 23 plus hours a day adding to the inhumanity of our punishment-based and racist prison system.

We know that we do not live in isolation. We are all part of a society in which these things exist, and we are all responsible to live our lives and make our choices in ways that will address the quality of life and justice in our communities. Of course, we want to make the world a better place, but it is all so overwhelming. How do we know what to do?

There is an old story that is sometimes told in social justice gatherings. There was a village on a river and one day people found some bodies floating down the river. Of course, they pulled them from the river and buried them, but the next day there were wounded people floating down the river. So the townspeople rescued them and built a hospital to heal them.

The bodies continued to come and the people continued to respond, creating social services to help the wounded and grieving people. One day, however, someone spoke up and said, "let's go up the river and find out why they are falling in."

The point of the story, of course, is that we must not only look to assist and heal the victims of society but look to the causes of the social conditions that cause poverty and violence and addiction, and work to change social structures. We need to do both things. We need to love and tend to the wounded (and to understand the degree to which we ourselves are wounded); and we need to examine and change the structures of our society to prevent the harm in the first place. We might think of social change as a patchwork quilt, many different people working in different areas in different ways according to their skills and passions. We need to work on our square of the quilt from the place of our own gifts.

But how? How do we know what to do? This is a matter of discernment. Are we go up the river people? Are we good at understanding structures, and/or good at working to change them? Are we good activists, happy and comfortable at challenging authorities and conventions?

Or perhaps we are better at taking care of the wounded, good at compassionately responding to people in trouble, able to create ways of helping and interacting with those who are the victims of violence or social inequities. Perhaps we are good at helping people to be healed of the long term wounds that are suffered in trauma. Maybe we're good at starting programs or organizations. Or maybe we're good at encouraging and supporting others in doing these things. Perhaps we've been fortunate economically and can employ, educate, and support others.

Jesus, in the extracanonical gospel of Thomas said, "If you bring forth what is within you, what you bring forth will save you." The first step, and a continuing periodic step, to making the world a better place is personal discernment. Where does God speak to you in your heart? What does God call you to do? You. Uniquely you, what does God want you to do? When you think of particular activities what lifts your heart? Don't do what others around you say that you should do, unless that feels right with you.

Bring forth what is within you – it will help to save the world. And then find organizations or others doing that thing and do it with them, whether it's working in a food pantry or lobbying at the state house, or protesting, or volunteering in prison or at a shelter, or creating new visions for how to do things, or writing or speaking to educate and inspire others. All of these things, and more, are important, so discern, choose, and do!

And while doing this, discerning your actions and commitments at particular times in your life, simply make extra efforts to be kind to your neighbors and to greet others in the street kindly, and to be compassionate in your daily interactions. The world needs our love in small ways as well as large.

Jesus told another of those confusing stories one day. A man gave several of his servants some coins (called talents) and went away on a trip. Two of the servants invested the coins that they had, but one who had been given only one coin was afraid of the responsibility and hid it to be safe. When the man returned, those who had used their coins had multiplied them. The man was pleased with them, but when he heard that one of the men had just hidden the talent in fear, he was very displeased. He took the one coin away and gave it to the others. We understood that even if we are uncertain of what we are to do, frightened of responsibility perhaps, it was better to take a chance and give it a try. (Imagined from Matt. 25:14-28)

EPILOGUE: TRY, WORK WITH OTHERS, TRY AGAIN, LOVE

It was after the sad events in Jerusalem, and Cleopas and I were walking along the road to Emmaus. We were trying to understand what had happened, thinking back through Jesus's entire ministry and our role as disciples. We had worked hard and sometimes we had done well and sometimes we had failed, but we kept trying, and loving. We marveled at the healing and feeding that Jesus did, and we tried to be good disciples and help with this. What did it all mean? Of course, now we felt that perhaps it was all in vain, that it meant nothing, since Jesus had been executed. Despite the crowds that followed him, despite the bold and transforming truth of love that he told, it seemed as if the Empire and its violent and dishonest ways had triumphed after all.

We were trying to understand all this when a stranger joined us. He heard of our disappointment, our confusion, and our fear, and he started to speak to us and to explain it all. He said that we should not lose hope, that the message was about a love that would not end or be defeated, that life and love would triumph over fear and hatred, that the kingdom was surely among us and even within us. Our hearts were warmed by his words, but we found them hard to understand.

When we arrived at Emmaus, we invited the stranger to join us for a meal. We chatted until the host brought some bread and wine to nourish us. The stranger took the bread, blessed it, and broke it and something astonishing happened in the breaking of the bread. Suddenly the stranger was transformed before our eyes, and he was no stranger. This was one who was an intimate friend. It was our crucified teacher, well and whole and breaking bread with us. And then as suddenly as we had seen his true identity, he disappeared completely. Just disappeared, no longer visible to us, but we were left transformed in hope and love.

Everything had changed. The one that we perceived to be dead was living. We had had a true vision, and everything would be different. The coming days would be challenging. We would lose faith sometimes, we would make mistakes, sometimes we would be depressed or feel defeated...but we knew that we had been transformed by a vision of the living Christ. Somehow, God was in the world with us, in our work, in our very being. Love would win. (Imagined from Luke 24:13-32)

I had several reasons for wanting to write this book. One of the reasons was to tell the stories, however briefly and inadequately, of beautiful people whom I encountered doing ministry, people who lived, sometimes suffered abuse or neglect or addiction and poverty, and in some cases died prematurely. Beautiful, vibrant, people who matter. Their lives matter. Their stories need to be told, even if just raised up to God as if in prayer. They lived. They had names and relationships and words and stories. I used pseudonyms in many cases to protect them but let me just say now that I have loved you -Kim, Danny, Mandy, Diane, Corrine, Elizabeth, Jesus, Maryann, Wanee, Pauline, Rosetta, Ann, Alim, Colus, April, Gwen, Leonard, Hattie, Lois, John C., Tony, George, John, Kim, Michael, Donna, Charles, Angela, Alfreda, Venus, I have seen you, you have mattered to me, and I celebrate you.

Without question, I have been transformed through these years, and I have been changed in my essence by each of those named above and many others whose lives have touched mine. This is a journey of faith that I have walked with others, privileged to share with them in their journeys, and all along the way I have been touched, sustained, guided by the spirit of Holy Mystery, God, the Holy spirit, God beyond God. That ineffable, eternal, transcendent Truth of love. It is also a journey of faith that I tell.

The theologian, teacher, and writer, Illia Delio said "I lived for God, God lived in them, and I lived in them, and they in me." (Delio 2019)

In 1975 I stepped into a classroom at Harvard Divinity School. The professor was Sr. Dr. Marie Augusta Neal, SNDdeN, the class was Religion and Society. The course work included liberation theology and in that encounter I was transformed by a Holy call. God spoke to me clearly and powerfully, and I hadn't the faintest idea what I would do, but I believed that call and God found a way.

I walked into a workshop at a district conference and met Scotty McLennan, and then into the Benevolent Fraternity (one day to be call the UU Urban Ministry) and met Bud Murdock, and I found myself with a space and a charge to start a shelter for women who had been abused or suffered another crisis. How would I do such a thing? I networked and met people and the community grew and we did it together. The Spirit was there with us, finding a way where there seemed no way.

During this time, I was not only a minister; I was a mother. I was raising two beautiful children in the city, and I didn't know how to do that. But God provided compassionate wise others to support us, and Lee and Rachel grew into wise and compassionate people themselves. They, along with grandchildren, continue to be the joy of my life.

I ministered with seriously mentally ill people, and situations of violence, and kidnapping, poverty and despair. I didn't know how to minister in such circumstances. But the Spirit said to keep loving, and keep trying, and work with others, and do your best. And trusting in the Spirit and looking to others, I would find a way.

Then I was director of an agency; I didn't know how to do that. The spirit within me said to seek the kingdom of God first and I prayed and realized that this was how it always was. First, love God and neighbor with heart soul and mind, do your best, work with others, and the way would become clear.

Children started shooting each other in the neighborhood of our Roxbury church and we wanted to save them, and we didn't know how, but we opened the church, and the youth came in, and some of them were violent and all of them were scared and the world was crazy and we took them in and loved them. We built a program step by step, even though we didn't know how, but we loved them and worked with each other.

The clarity of my call grew through these years of loving and trying. I was led ever more deeply into a Jesus path, influenced by Ignatian spiritual direction, Catholic and other Christian friends on the front line, my own heart informed by my childhood faith and the many people I had loved in the ministry. Co-pastoring a church with Graylan, a church with a deliberate liberation theology message, and a congregation full of recovering substance abusers and activists, further allowed the Spirit to move in my heart and my life as I came to know more brave people. There was that wonderful tradition of the Christian Church (Disciples of Christ), to experience communion every Sunday, circling up, remembering Jesus and "all who had fallen in the struggle for justice": passing the bread from one to another; drinking juice from a common cup—always juice in honor of loved ones in recovery.

Graylan was called to church in D.C., and we tried a commuter marriage, but sadly, it did not work out and we parted. I lived alone. I heard shots in the night, there were break-ins to my home, and a bullet through my own wall. There were crises in the community and crises in the programs and I looked for comfort in the wrong place, could not say no to a disordered relationship. I failed and hurt people and lost my beloved ministry.

I didn't know what to do next, and how to heal the pain and the shame that I felt, but I looked to God, and I was held up by friends and family. I deeply regretted my error and I tried to learn and to deepen spiritually. I spent almost a year in prayer and in study as I looked for what to do next, and I kept loving.

God found a way for me, and I moved to another state where I was privileged to love and to worship in the manner of Friends (Quakers). I was charged with starting a program for at-risk youth in a very poor post-industrialized city. I networked and worked with others and loved, and started a program for adjudicated youth and witnessed more violence and loss among more incredibly beautiful souls. I was further transformed by them.

Finally, I retired, but was briefly called part time to a UU church that embraced me and reminded me of all those good UU values and people that had inspired me along the way. It was reconciliation. At the same time, I found a Jesuit community, The Spiritual Direction Center at Wernersville, Pennsylvania, where I studied spiritual direction and deepened in the Ignatian ways, directing others to find God in all things. My heart was fully Christian by then and I found an Episcopal church that captured my heart, and I moved into Philadelphia, another beloved city, where I rejoice in the beauty of my community and the honor that it is to be among so many unique people who transform me daily.

I have engaged in many different activities since I have

been in Philly, and I will continue. I don't know what I will do next, or how to do it, but I know that I live in the abundance of God's love, and I am eternally grateful; that I will continue to learn from others; and that I will keep trying to love.

"The pursuit of holiness is learning to integrate the threads of our many loves into the single-hearted love of God. 'You truly exist where you love' St. Bonaventure wrote, 'not merely where you live.' Where we grow in love is where we find our true being because it is where we find our freedom; and where we find our freedom is where we grow into our true identity in God." (Illia Delio P.14, *Birth of a Dancing Star*)

It was not the last time we were to see Jesus. For a number of days he would appear to some of the disciples and then be gone again. One day we were at the beach preparing bread and fruit and other food for Peter and the others because they had been out fishing all night. We had a fire going for the fish that we were hoping they would bring in. And then he was among us, again. Jesus, our teacher. Or was he the risen Christ, ushering in a kingdom of God? Real? Embodied? Transcendent? He seemed so down to earth, but how could he be here at all, and what was with this appearing and disappearing thing. We were never sure in those amazing times.

Of course, as he had done in the past, Jesus told the disciples where to find fish so that their nets were overflowing. And we all had a feast that early morning.

It seemed from his remarks that Jesus was planning to leave us soon in any worldly form and wanted to give us final instructions. They were simple. They were basic. They were clear, if difficult to accomplish. Feed my sheep, he said. If you love me, feed my sheep, tend my lambs, if you love me, care for the sheep. In other words, if you love me, love one another. (Imagined from John 21:1-17)

REFERENCES

Buechner, Frederick. 1993. *Whistling in the Dark: A Doubter's Dictionary.* San Francisco: HarperSanFrancisco.

Delio, Illia. 2019. *Birth of a Dancing Star, My Journey from Cradle Catholic to Cyborg Christian.* Orbis Books.

Fowler, James W. 1995. *Stages of Faith, the Psychology of Human Development and the Quest for Meaning.* HarperOne.

Hafiz. 1996. *I Heard God Laughing: Poems of Hope and Joy.* New York: Penguin Books.

Johnson, Elizabeth A. 2007. *Quest for the Living God, Mapping Frontiers in the Theology of God.* Continuum.

Morrison, Toni. 2015. "No Place for Self-Pity, No Room for Fear." *The Nation,* March 23.

Spivak, Deborah Prothrow Smith and Howard R. 2003. *Murder Is No Accident: Understanding and Preventing Youth Violence in America.* Jossey-Bass.

Made in the USA
Middletown, DE
11 August 2024

58407694R10142